The Complete Guide to
Creating Your Own Living Trust

A Step-by-Step Plan to Protect Your Assets, Limit Your Taxes, and Ensure Your Wishes are Fulfilled

By Steven D. Fisher

The Complete Guide to Creating Your Own Living Trust: A Step-by-Step Plan to
Protect Your Assets, Limit Your Taxes, and Ensure Your Wishes are Fulfilled

Copyright © 2008 by Atlantic Publishing Group, Inc.
1405 SW 6th Ave. • Ocala, Florida 34471 • 800-814-1132 • 352-622-1875–Fax
Web site: www.atlantic-pub.com • E-mail: sales@atlantic-pub.com
SAN Number: 268-1250

ISBN-13: 978-1-60138-113-2   ISBN-10: 1-60138-113-1

Library of Congress Cataloging-in-Publication Data

Fisher, Steven D., 1944-
  The complete guide to creating your own living trust : a step by step plan to protect your
assets, limit your taxes, and ensure your wishes are fulfilled / By Steven D. Fisher.
     p. cm.
  ISBN-13: 978-1-60138-113-2 (alk. paper)
  ISBN-10: 1-60138-113-1 (alk. paper)
 1. Living trusts--United States--Popular works. 2. Estate planning--United States--Popular
works. I. Title.

 KF734.F57 2008
 346.7305'2--dc22
                                   2008022348

Printed on Recycled Paper

INTERIOR LAYOUT DESIGN: Nicole Deck ndeck@atlantic-pub.com

Printed in the United States

We recently lost our beloved pet "Bear," who was not only our best and dearest friend but also the "Vice President of Sunshine" here at Atlantic Publishing. He did not receive a salary but worked tirelessly 24 hours a day to please his parents. Bear was a rescue dog that turned around and showered myself, my wife Sherri, his grandparents Jean, Bob and Nancy and every person and animal he met (maybe not rabbits) with friendship and love. He made a lot of people smile every day.

We wanted you to know that a portion of the profits of this book will be donated to The Humane Society of the United States.

–*Douglas & Sherri Brown*

THE HUMANE SOCIETY
OF THE UNITED STATES ©

The human-animal bond is as old as human history. We cherish our animal companions for their unconditional affection and acceptance. We feel a thrill when we glimpse wild creatures in their natural habitat or in our own backyard.

Unfortunately, the human-animal bond has at times been weakened. Humans have exploited some animal species to the point of extinction.

The Humane Society of the United States makes a difference in the lives of animals here at home and worldwide. The HSUS is dedicated to creating a world where our relationship with animals is guided by compassion. We seek a truly humane society in which animals are respected for their intrinsic value, and where the human-animal bond is strong.

Want to help animals? We have plenty of suggestions. Adopt a pet from a local shelter, join The Humane Society and be a part of our work to help companion animals and wildlife. You will be funding our educational, legislative, investigative and outreach projects in the U.S. and across the globe.

Or perhaps you'd like to make a memorial donation in honor of a pet, friend or relative? You can through our Kindred Spirits program. And if you'd like to contribute in a more structured way, our Planned Giving Office has suggestions about estate planning, annuities, and even gifts of stock that avoid capital gains taxes.

Maybe you have land that you would like to preserve as a lasting habitat for wildlife. Our Wildlife Land Trust can help you. Perhaps the land you want to share is a backyard—that's enough. Our Urban Wildlife Sanctuary Program will show you how to create a habitat for your wild neighbors.

So you see, it's easy to help animals. And The HSUS is here to help.

The Humane Society of the United States
2100 L Street NW
Washington, DC 20037
202-452-1100
www.hsus.org

Table of Contents

Chapter 3: How Do Living Trusts Affect Your Taxes? 29

Chapter 4: Who Are the Parties to a Trust? 51

Chapter 7: Who are the Beneficiaries of a Living Trust? 101

Chapter 8: How Do I Leave Property to Minor Children or Young Adults?........109

Chapter 9: What Are the Responsibilities of the Successor Trustee?........................123

Chapter 10: How Do I Transfer Property to My Living Trust?...............................135

Chapter 11: What Happens After the Grantor Dies? 137

Chapter 12: What Other Methods of Probate Avoidance Are There? 145

1
What is a Living Trust?

A trust is a legal arrangement by which property is given to one person (the trustee) to manage for the benefit of a third person. A living (or inter vivos) trust gets its name from the fact that the trust goes into effect while the trust creator is still living. Although there are numerous elements to a trust, a living trust contains a minimum of two documents:

- Declaration of Trust and Articles of Trust — This is the first step in creating a living trust. Once it is written and signed, your trust exists.

- Pour-Over Will — This is an instrument that ensures that property not transferred to your living trust will be left ("poured over") to that trust upon your death.*

*Note: *There is disagreement among trust experts about the need for a pour-over will for a living trust. Critics argue that such wills do not avoid probate. Probate can cause the living trust to go on for months rather than being settled quickly — one of the main advantages of a living trust.*

There are other documents included — Durable Power of Attorney for General Assets, Durable Power of Attorney for Health, and others. These items will be discussed in more detail later.

What Is the Purpose of a Living Trust?

The basic purpose of a living trust is to provide an easy way to transfer property upon your death. It also provides an excellent way to avoid the costs and complications of the probate process. In probate the estate of a deceased person is settled by the courts. The court resolves all claims and distributes the decedent's property. Probate is a public process. Trust property — unlike probate — passes directly to your designated beneficiaries without any court involvement. It is private. People prefer the privacy, convenience, and lower cost of a living trust arrangement to the drawn-out and expensive probate process.

How Did the Living Trust Evolve?

The history of the living trust is a long and complicated one with origins in Greek and Roman law (and other cultures because inheritance of wealth is a universal topic). It is a complicated subject and not within the scope of this book. However, in basic terms of English and American law, the trust developed in England during the era of the Crusades. It was known as the use of land. Landowners were recruited to fight in the Crusades. While they were gone, a person was required to manage their estates and to pay and receive feudal dues. Friends would be selected, and ownership of lands would be conveyed to them with the understanding that the land would be returned to the

"Crusader" on his return. However, at that time, English law viewed the person with whom the land had been left as the only owner. So upon return, the original owner had no claim to it. This did not sit well with the returned landowner, so he did the only thing he could do — petition the king. As a matter of routine, the monarch would turn the matter over to the Lord Chancellor, who would decide the case. Eventually the Chancellor's court recognized that the returning landowner held true claim to his property, and that the "legal owner" (the trustee) held the land only for the benefit of the original owner and had to turn it over to him upon request. Over the centuries, this definition evolved into the modern concept of the trust. So, today, property of any sort (land, stock, bonds, and other assets) can be held "in trust" for another person.

What Are the Advantages of a Living Trust?

A living trust helps you avoid the cost and inconvenience of probate. Any property that passes outside probate incurs no probate fees, so you avoid expensive fees by using a living trust. Probate proceedings can also take months or years to be completed, denying your beneficiaries access to their property. (See Chapter 2 for more details on probate.) This does not happen with a living trust, as the property passes immediately to the beneficiaries. Such a trust has several other advantages:

- If you are a married couple and set the trust up in the correct manner, you can double the estate tax exemption amount (the amount of net worth above which an estate tax is levied).

· If you are incapacitated, you can provide for uninterrupted management of the trust property. You can also avoid interruption of management at death.

· If you support charities, you can pass property to charity and save taxes at death.

· A trust can be revised, amended, or revoked for any reason at any time before your death as long as you are legally competent.* You can easily adapt it to fit changing financial and personal circumstances.

*"Competent" means you possess the mental capacity to make and understand decisions concerning your property. Through court proceedings, a person can be declared legally "incompetent." Although it is rare, this court proceeding can occur when a person challenges the mental competence of the grantor to make, revoke, or amend a living trust.

A trust is more difficult to contest than a will, reducing the threat of future legal action. Unlike a will, which only goes into effect upon the death of a person (and not until a probate court allows it), a living trust goes into effect as it is created and assets are placed in it. The settlor (person creating the trust) sets up the trust with full knowledge and control. This makes it difficult for a person to launch a lawsuit claiming that the settlor lacked capacity, was unduly influenced by others to set up the trust, or that the trust was improperly executed. Another guard against lawsuits is that whoever is doing the suing (the "contestant") has no power over the disposition of the assets. In other words, the contestant cannot tie up the assets while attacking the trust. The trust beneficiaries can enjoy the trust benefits while the lawsuit is pursued; the contestant can waste money and time and end up with little or nothing. This is in stark contrast to the contesting of a will where the contestant can tie the assets of the estate into legal knots for years, while preventing beneficiaries from getting the full enjoyment and use of the property. In this case, the estate has an incentive to settle with a contestant just to get rid of him or her so they can begin enjoying the property.

There is one more benefit in this area of living trusts. You can increase your protection by including an anti-contest provision in your trust as well as your will. In other words, you can make bequests to beneficiaries with the condition they not contest or attack the trust. The effect is to discourage any future legal action by giving the beneficiaries something tangible and valuable to lose.

What Are the Disadvantages of a Living Trust?

A living trust has disadvantages as well as advantages. It will not save you money on estate or state inheritance taxes. It can also be more expensive and complicated to set up than a will, but this is offset by eliminating probate fees. In addition, the expense is immediate and not after your death. Another disadvantage is that your property must be transferred to the trust; this results in minor complications in terms of rewriting and recording real estate deeds. Also, if someone other than yourself is the trustee, you may need to pay an annual trustee's fee. Fees can also occur at the time of termination. Finally, there are no immediate tax advantages to a trust. The disadvantages of a living trust are offset compared to the costs and complications of probate.

Who Should Have a Living Trust?

Anyone who wants to avoid probate can create a living trust. If you are a person with a significant amount of property, you will want a living trust. If you are elderly, seriously ill, or just plain prudent, a living trust may also be the choice for you. It may not a good option for you if you are young and in good health. It is also not a good choice if you are in debt because a living trust does not have a cut-off period in which creditors can file claims (unlike probate). With a trust, your creditors can lay claim to your assets over a much longer time. States may have streamlined probate procedures making probate a better choice than a living trust. If you are separated but not yet divorced, a living trust may not be a viable option. States may have rules about what can and cannot be done with property before a divorce decree is finalized. If you own little property, a living trust is not a good choice, either. In this case, probate will not cost that much.

How Much Does a Living Trust Cost?

This is a difficult question to answer since there is no hard and fast rule, and regulations vary state by state. You can save money by using the information in this book to create your own living trust. However, if you have considerable and complicated assets, it is best to use a professional who specializes in this area. According to Henry W. Abts III (The Living Trust, 2003), the cost for a revocable trust will range from $1,395 to $2,195, depending on the nature and complexity of the trust. According to **www.Kiplinger.com**, "a revocable living trust might add $750 to $2,000 to a married couple's plan that also includes a pour-over will and durable powers of attorney for financial matters and health care." Fees vary, thus the need to do careful research and be clear on what services they will provide. The lawyer should be able to explain the process to you in plain English. Beware of any lawyer who charges absurdly low fees and tries to confuse you with legal jargon. Typical services a lawyer should provide and charge for include:

- Review of your assets and their present title.

- Discussion of your estate plan with you.

- Preparation of your living trust, your will, and any related documents.

- Provision of services or instructions to fund your living trust.

2
Why All the Fuss About Avoiding Probate?

The term "probate" comes from the Latin word "probtum" meaning "prove." The probate is a legal process by which it is proved that a will is or is not genuine. Although specific procedures may vary by state, probate may include the following actions:

- When you die, your will is filed with the local probate court (also called a "surrogate" or "chancery" court).

- An inventory is taken of your property.

- The property is appraised for its value.

- If the will is determined valid in court, any legal debts (including death taxes) must be paid.

- After debts and fees are paid, the property is distributed as dictated by the will.

If the will is deemed not valid or if there is no will, the estate still must go through an "intestacy" (without a will) proceeding.

In this proceeding, the property is distributed to the closest relatives as dictated by state law.

A Brief History of Probate

English law is the origin of our system of probate. The ability to determine the validity of a will in court originated with the English ecclesiastical courts during the Middle Ages. At that time, religious courts had jurisdiction over succession to personal property, but the idea of probate had not reached the secular courts, which had jurisdiction over the descent of real property. England introduced a three-part probate system:

· Common law

· Ecclesiastical — personal property

· Equity — fiduciary property

That system has since been revised and modernized in England. According to critics, American law evolved and lumped the three-court system into one expensive and time consuming process called the "probate court."

Efforts to modernize the complex U.S. probate system have been attempted but little change has taken place. Below is a summary of the advantages and disadvantages of the current system.

Advantages of the Probate System

The probate system has its defenders. They point out the following advantages:

- Probate makes sure that only your beneficiaries receive your property. In other words, it prevents fraud. Creditors have to prove their claims against the estate.

- The probate process can resolve any disputes involving your estate and disposition of your assets.

- The probate process limits the time creditors have to make claims against the estate. There is a "statute of limitations." If creditors do not make their claims within the specified time period, they are out of luck, as their claims are no longer enforceable.

Disadvantages of the Probate System

Critics of the probate system say it has several disadvantages that make a living trust (and other probate-avoidance methods) an attractive alternative. Here is a summary of critics' comments:

- It can cost an excessive amount of money for the services rendered. Critics point out that property may be transferred within a close circle of family and friends. They also point out that estates are rarely dogged by creditors' claims. Probate then provides no real benefit, except to provide lawyers with lucrative fees. A 1990 study by the American Association of Retired Persons (AARP) titled *Probate: Consumer Perspectives and Concerns* reached sobering conclusions regarding the costs of probate. It concluded that the probate process can generate legal fees of 12 to 20 percent of the estate for the lawyer. It also concluded that probate can reduce the estate passing to one's heirs by 5 percent or more. Costs are involved in the area of the "executor." He or she is the person you appoint in your will to take on the responsibility of supervising your estate and ensuring that the terms of the will are followed. To read about AARP's perspective on the probate process, visit **http://dickhorgan.com/TrustandEstate.html** where you'll find complete information on a study of how the process works in the United States.

- If you die without a will, the courts will appoint an administrator to serve the same function as an executor. The executor then hires a probate lawyer to do the paperwork. The executor does little more than sign the necessary papers under the lawyer's directions. Both executor and lawyer are then entitled to a fee, which can be considerable, from your probate estate. The court may decide what fees are reasonable. In other states the fees are based on a percentage of the estate. Fees may also be based on gross probate estate. Additional costs may include court costs, appraiser's fees, and others. Also, basic fees may be set by statute. In addition, if "extraordinary" services are performed, the attorney or executor can ask for additional fees.

- Probate is primarily a clerical and administrative skill. Due to this, critics say there is no need for court proceedings or the legal and adversarial skills of a lawyer. They claim the process is normally handled by the lawyer's secretary or by a probate form preparation company. When this happens, your beneficiaries end up paying far in excess of the services rendered.

· Probate proceedings consume too much time. On average, a typical probate proceeding can take between one and two years. During that time, your beneficiaries basically get nothing or perhaps only a "family allowance" dictated by a judge. Perhaps the most famous "worst case" scenario involved Marilyn Monroe's estate. It went through probate for 18 years and is claimed to be the longest in American history. During that time, an estate estimated at between $800,000 and $1.6 million was decimated by taxes and attorneys' fees. By the time probate was completed, all her heirs had left was about $100,000.

Supporters and critics of the probate process have valid points. However, advocates may indulge in overheated rhetoric to support their positions. It is important to not get caught up in the emotional claims and counter-claims. Keep an objective mind on the topic and choose the right legal method for your particular situation. This book is concerned with the living trust. However, there are other methods of avoiding probate, including (in alphabetical order):

· Exemption of certain small amounts of property left by will from probate (depends on state)

· Gifts made while you are alive

· Joint tenancy or tenancy by the entirety

- Life insurance

- Pay-on-death financial accounts

- Retirement accounts

- Transfer on-death registration for stocks and bonds

How Do You Know If You Need or Do Not Need a Living Trust?

If you are elderly, seriously ill, or simply want to take the common-sense approach of avoiding probate, then a living trust is a good idea for you. In addition, if you own a significant amount of property, then a living trust is a good choice.

On the other hand, it is likely you do not need a living trust if it makes more sense to use a different probate-avoidance method. If you are young and in good health, you also do not need a living trust. It is unlikely at this stage of life that you would die suddenly or that you own a significant amount of property. In this case, a will may be a better and less expensive choice than a living trust. Save the trust for when you are older and have acquired a larger amount of property.

A living trust is also not a good idea if you have significant and complicated debt problems. There is no cutoff period with a trust. Creditors have more time to lay claim to your assets than with probate, which has a definite cutoff period. Probate procedures may have been streamlined. If you live in one of those states, then probate may be a better choice than a living trust. However, you will need to check and compare costs.

If you are separated but not yet divorced a living trust is also not a good idea. Your state may have rules about what you can and cannot do with your property before the divorce is final.

A living trust also does not make much sense when you have little property or other assets. In this case, probate will not cost much and will be cheaper and less complicated than a trust. You should not use a living trust to name a personal guardian to care for your minor children, either. This is a function of a will.

3
How Do Living Trusts Affect Your Taxes?

T axes cannot be avoided. However, with a living trust you can reduce your tax burden significantly. There are four areas of taxes that you need to be familiar with in terms of your estate and a living trust.

The Federal Estate Tax

The estate tax is a federal tax imposed on your estate as a whole upon your death or in anticipation of death (including transfers made two years prior to death). Your executor completes a single estate tax return, and he or she pays the tax out of the estate's funds. Only if the executor fails to pay the tax are the heirs held liable for the tax. Estate taxes exemptions can change. Congress is involved, and exemptions are subject to the winds of political weather. At present, as a result of the Economic Growth and Tax Relief Reconciliation Act of 2001, the estate tax exemption varies by year as shown in the table below.

Year	Estate Tax Exemption	Gift Tax Emption	Estate & Gift Tax Rate (Highest)
2007	$2 million	$1 million	45%
2008	$2 million	$ 1 million	45%
2009	$3.5 million	$1 million	45%
2010	No estate tax	$1 million	35% (gift tax only)
2011	$1 million	$1 million	55%

As an example, if you died in 2008 and your entire estate values $1.9 million, no estate taxes are levied because it is less than the $2 million exemption. Remember, these exemptions are personal ones. If you are a married couple, you can exempt twice the amount in your estate — $4 million in 2007 and 2008 and $7 million in 2009. Federal estate taxes (as well as any state estate taxes) are due within nine months of a person's death. However, you can request an automatic six-month exemption. As stated above, these exemptions may change so it is important to keep abreast of any Congressional revisions or other changes so you can adapt and modify your estate and living will plans accordingly.

State Taxes

Unlike the federal government, state governments can impose both inheritance and estate taxes. Inheritance taxes are imposed by states on the property beneficiaries receive from estates. The tax is paid by your estate before any assets are distributed. The inheritance tax may be figured separately for each beneficiary, which means each beneficiary is responsible for paying his or her own inheritance taxes. Those states that have inheritance taxes may tax spouses and children of the deceased at lower rates than other heirs. As of this writing, ten states still collect an inheritance tax. They are: Connecticut, Indiana, Iowa, Kansas, Kentucky, Maryland, Nebraska, New Jersey, Pennsylvania, and Tennessee. States with no inheritance tax or only a pickup tax are:

- Alabama
- Alaska
- Arizona
- Arkansas
- California
- Colorado
- District of Columbia
- Florida
- Georgia
- Hawaii
- Idaho
- Illinois
- Maine
- Massachusetts
- Michigan
- Minnesota
- Missouri
- Nevada
- New Mexico
- North Dakota
- Oregon
- Rhode Island
- South Carolina
- Texas
- Utah
- Vermont
- Virginia
- Washington
- West Virginia
- Wisconsin
- Wyoming

A pickup tax is a method whereby states "pick up" a portion of the estate tax owed to the federal government. Federal law was designed to eliminate state inheritance taxes by apportioning a part of the federal estate tax to the states. Its effect was to reduce the amount of inheritance taxes paid to states.

States still collecting inheritance taxes may allow five exemptions under their inheritance tax laws:

1. Personal exemptions

2. Specified exemption amounts for the whole estate

3. Property exemptions (property on which a tax has already been paid)

4. equests for charitable, educational, or religious institutions

5. Exemptions for specific kinds of property

Gift Taxes

You can reduce the value of your taxable estate by giving gifts, thus reducing the amount of taxes you have to pay. Thanks to the 2001 changes, the federal gift and estate tax were integrated into a unified tax system called the "unified credit." The unified credit is the total amount that federal law allows you to exempt from taxation. (See the end of the chapter for the Internal Revenue Service's rules on this subject.) In effect, it amounts to a credit against your federal estate taxes. "Gifting" is the transfer of any property without expecting anything in return. Gifts are taxable; however, as with any tax law, there are exceptions. The following gifts are not taxable under current law:

- The first $12,000 you give to someone in the same year (the annual exclusion)

- Medical expenses or tuition you pay for someone (the educational and medical exclusion)

- Gifts to your spouse who is a U.S. citizen

- Gifts to political organizations

- Gifts to tax-exempt charities

A separate $12,000 annual exclusion is available for each person you gift. This means you can give $12,000 each year to a number of people, charities, or organizations, and all these gifts are free of taxes. If you are a married couple, you can give away $24,000 tax-free. Also, the current annual exclusion figure can rise since it is pegged to the Consumer Price Index and inflation figures. If the government decides to increase the annual exclusion, it does so in $1,000 increments.

Remember from the table earlier in this chapter there is a $1 million gift exemption. This exemption refers to the total number of gifts you give away during your lifetime. If you gift individuals or organizations with $12,000 (or another amount) over the years, it will eventually reach $1 million. After you exceed that exemption figure, you will pay a gift tax on any gifts you provide. The reason for this restriction is simple. Without it, people with large estates would simply gift their estates over their lifetimes. This would reduce the estates down to the exemption level, and they would end up paying no taxes. The federal government may be bureaucratic, but it is not unintelligent, so it placed a limit on the exemption.

As with any bureaucracy, there are forms to be filled out. In terms of the gift tax, you will need to complete IRS Form 709 in the following instances:

· If you give more than $12,000 during the year to someone other than your spouse.

· If you and your spouse are splitting the gift. This occurs when you and your spouse give a gift to a person or organization, and half of that gift is considered made by you and half by your spouse. According to IRS regulations, you have to file a return even if your half of the gift is less than $12,000.

· If you provide someone other than your spouse with a gift that he or she cannot possess, enjoy, or derive income from until sometime in the future.

· If you give your spouse an interest in property that will end by a future decision or event.

Gifting is an option available to everyone, but of course it works best for those who have the assets to work with — those people with large estates. For these individuals it is best to gift over a long time to reduce the value of the estate and reap the benefit of reduced taxes.

Income Taxes

In terms of income taxes, it is important to remember that estates are taxed, not your heirs. This means that when beneficiaries inherit the assets of your estate, they do not have to report those assets as income for tax purposes. But if they receive income-generating assets (for example, rental properties, securities accounts, and other income producers), then that income must be included on their personal income tax returns. If those assets continue to generate income for the heirs over the years, that income must also be accounted for on personal income tax returns.

An estate's income must be reported annually. This may be either on a calendar year or fiscal year basis. A fiscal tax year is any period that ends on the last day of a month and does not exceed 12 months. The executor or successor trustee may pick the estate's accounting period when filing the first income tax return by the April 15 deadline (in the case of an extension, by October 15). On the return, the IRS taxes the annual net income earning by your trust (or estate). Any income a deceased person had a right to receive is included in the estate and is subject to estate tax. This income is also taxed by the IRS when received by the estate or beneficiary. In the latter case, however, there is an income tax deduction allowed for the recipient for the estate tax paid on the income.

Tax Breaks

Under current tax code, significant breaks are given to married couples and traditional families. When they file their own income tax returns, survivors can qualify for specified benefits. Here is one example: A surviving spouse can file a joint return for the year of death and may qualify for special tax rates for the next two years. Here is another example: If the deceased qualified as your dependent (someone under your care, such as a minor) during part of the year before death, you are allowed to claim the dependent exemption. This is regardless of when the death occurred during the year. Here is one more example: If your spouse died within the two tax years preceding the year in which your return is being filed, you may be eligible to claim the filing status of widow or widower with a dependent child. This qualifies you to use the tax rates for married filing jointly. When you meet all the following requirements, you may qualify for this benefit:

- You were entitled to file a joint return with your spouse for the year of death, whether or not you filed jointly.

- You did not re-marry prior to the end of the current tax year.

- You have a child, stepchild, or foster child qualifying as your dependent for the tax year.

- You supply more than half the cost of maintaining your home (the principal place of residence).

Dealing with taxes after the death of a loved one is not easy and may be the last thing on your mind in a highly emotional situation. For that reason, you may want to use the services of a professional who can relieve you of that burden. In terms of trusts, the paperwork is relatively simple, but it still may not be something you or your spouse wants to deal with. Seek help if necessary.

Another tax break comes in the form of the unlimited marital deduction. Current law allows a spouse to leave any amount of property to the surviving spouse free of estate tax, no matter what the value of the property. As always, there is a catch.

You can leave the bulk of your assets to your spouse, and that transfer of is free of taxes. But, if you leave your assets to your spouse, that increases the amount of the estate to him or her, and that means the estate may not be entirely exempt. This in turn means taxes will be due upon the death of the surviving spouse. This is a problem faced by couples who have no trusts or no will. So you can will all your assets to your spouse upon your death and use the unlimited marital deduction, but after your spouse dies, estate taxes will need to be paid if the value of the estate totals more than the allowable deductions.

Here is an example: Joe and Barbara share an estate valued at $5 million. Joe dies in 2007, leaving his assets to Barbara. Under the marital deduction, no estate tax is due. In this situation, both Joe and Barbara planned to leave their assets to their two children. Let us assume Barbara dies in 2009, and the estate has appreciated to $5.5 million. The 2009 personal exemption is $3.5 million. That means $2 million is now subject to the estate tax. The net result — the children receive less money when the estate tax is paid.

The unlimited marital deduction applies only to married couples. Life partners, whether gay, lesbian, or heterosexual, cannot use this deduction. This also applies if a partner is not a U.S. citizen. You do, however, have options in terms of gifts and exemptions. For example, you can provide your non-citizen spouse with a total of $112,000 annually without any gift or estate tax implications. Both of you can still make use of your personal gift tax exemptions. A third method to employ is the Qualified Domestic Trust (QDOT). This trust allows married couples to transfer assets between themselves at death without subjecting those assets to the federal estate tax. The caveat is that at least one trustee of a QDOT must be a U.S. citizen or a domestic corporation, such as a bank or trust company. The QDOT trust document also must stipulate that no distribution can be made from the trust unless the trustee has the right to withhold federal estate taxes from the distribution.

As we will see in later chapters, trusts can help you avoid the "second tax." This refers to the tax on the estate of the surviving trust. A later chapter will also provide specifics on developing an estate plan. First we will learn about the complicated subject of stepped-up valuation basis to see how it affects trusts, your estate, and taxes.

Stepped-Up Valuation

This concept has its roots in the 1981 Tax Reform Act. It refers to the stepped-up valuation of property, real estate property in particular. The goal of the act was to introduce fairness in the taxation of estates. At the core of stepped-up valuation is the stepped-up basis. "Basis" concerns how much you can profit from the sale of an asset. Although any asset is subject to stepped-up valuation, we will use real estate (a house) as an example for our explanation of basis. Here is the formula for figuring basis:

Purchase Price of House

+ $ Spent on Improvements

- (Depreciation)

= Basis

Assume you bought the house for $200,000. Then you added

$50,000 worth of capital improvements (added a wing, made cosmetic improvements). later, you sell the house for $450,000 due to appreciation and market conditions. (There was no depreciation.) Using our formula for determining basis:

$200,000 purchase price

+ 50,000 capital improvements

= $250,000 basis

Your taxable profit is $200,000 ($450,000 - $250,000).

This gives your inheritors of real estate a break in the following way. Assume you die before selling the house and your son or daughter inherits the house used in the above example. Your child inherits the property at the $450,000 market value, not $250,000. If he or she sells the house quickly at $450,000, there is no taxable profit. This is a simplified example and does not explore all the ins and outs of stepped-up valuation. If you want to know more, contact a tax professional who is well-versed in this area. However, there is one other area we need to explore before moving on to the subject of parties to a trust — community property states versus non-community property states and how stepped-up valuation is affected by the laws of these states.

In non-community property states, any property owned by a married individual receives a stepped-up basis upon his or her death. The surviving spouse's property, however, is not eligible for the stepped-up basis. According to IRS regulations, if you and your spouse hold property in joint tenancy, then when the first spouse dies, the surviving spouse can only get a stepped-up basis on the half of the property owned by the deceased spouse. The half owned by the surviving spouse does not get a new stepped-up basis. So if that property is later sold, the property suffers more tax if it has gone up in value after the creation of the joint tenancy but before the first spouse became deceased. However, the other half of the property will get a stepped-up valuation upon the death of the second spouse (if the property was not sold before then). This means that any children who inherit that property will also inherit the new basis.

In community property states, where each spouse owns one-half interest in shared property, both halves of property of the spouses receive a stepped-up basis upon the death of one spouse. So if you are a surviving spouse, you get a higher stepped-up basis on a home. The result is that capital gains are significantly lower, and any taxes due on the subsequent sale of that home are also reduced. In effect, when the stepped-up basis on a home or other real property rises, the taxes owed on the sale of the property decline. As of this writing, there are nine community property states: Arizona, California, Idaho, Louisiana, Nevada, New Mexico, Texas, Washington, and Wisconsin.

There is an obvious tax advantage to living in a community property state. Several non-community states recognized this and have passed statutes to institute community property laws (Wisconsin was the first). If you happen to be one of the many Americans who moves from state to state, you can take advantage of community property laws by transferring your assets into a living trust in a community property state and receive full stepped-up valuation even if you later move to a non-community state. If you currently live in a non-community property state and own property in joint tenancy, you have the ability to transfer your property into a living trust as a "tenancy in common in equal shares." In this case, it may be necessary for you to transfer your title from "joint tenancy" to "tenancy in common in equal shares." If you do not, the IRS may view the property as still being held in joint tenancy within the living trust and require you to abide by joint tenancy restrictions (such as being required to leave your property share to the joint tenant upon your death).

There is no doubt about it — taxes are a complicated subject, and no one enjoys paying taxes. However, by understanding the material in this book and planning carefully, you can certainly minimize the amount you owe the federal government. If you have the time and patience, you can learn the details of the tax code and benefit from the knowledge you gain. However, if you would rather not deal with a complicated subject, consult a certified public accountant or other tax profe.

Unified Credit (Applicable Exclusion Amount)

The following information is adapted from IRS Publication 950, which can be accessed online at **www.irs.gov/publications/ p950/ar02.html#d0e305**.

A credit is an amount that eliminates or reduces tax. A unified credit applies to both the gift tax and the estate tax. You must subtract the unified credit from any gift tax that you owe. Any unified credit you use against your gift tax in one year reduces the amount of credit that you can use against your gift tax in a later year. The total amount used during life against your gift tax reduces the credit available to use against your estate tax.

The unified credit against taxable gifts will remain at $345,800 (exempting $1 million from tax) through 2009, while the unified credit against estate tax increases during the same period. The following table shows the unified credit and applicable exclusion amount for the calendar years in which a gift is made or a decedent dies after 2001.

| Year | For Gift Tax Purposes | | For Estate Tax Purposes | |
	Unified Credit	Applicable Exclusion Amount	Unified Credit	Applicable Exclusion Amount
2006, 2007, and 2008	$345,800	$1,000,000	$780,800	$2,000,000
2009	$345,800	$1,000,000	$1,455,800	$3,500,000

Gift Tax

The gift tax applies to transfers by gift of any property. You make a gift if you give property, including money or the use of or income from property, without expecting to receive something of at least equal value in return. If you sell something at less than its full value or if you make an interest-free or reduced-interest loan, you may be making a gift. The general rule is that any gift is a taxable gift. However, there are exceptions to this rule. The following gifts are not taxable gifts:

· Gifts that are not more than the annual exclusion for the calendar year

· Tuition or medical expenses you pay directly to a medical or educational institution for someone

- Gifts to your spouse

- Gifts to a political organization for its use

- Gifts to charities

Annual Exclusion

A separate annual exclusion applies to each person to whom you make a gift. For 2006, the annual exclusion was $12,000. Therefore you and our spouse could each give up to $12,000 each to any number of people in 2006 and none of the gifts would have been taxable. If one of you gives more than $12,000 to a person in 2006, then gift splitting is involved (see below). However, gifts of future interests cannot be excluded under the annual exclusion provisions. A gift of a future interest is a gift that is limited so that its use, possession, or enjoyment will begin in the future.

Inflation adjustment

The annual exclusion may be increased due to cost-of-living adjustments. See the instructions for Form 709 for the amount of the annual exclusion for the year you make the gift.

- **Example 1**: In 2006 you give your niece a cash gift of $8,000. It is your only gift to her this year. The gift is not a taxable gift because it is not more than the $12,000 annual exclusion.

- **Example 2**: You pay the $15,000 college tuition of your friend. Because the payment qualifies for the educational exclusion, the gift is not a taxable gift.

· **Example 3.** In 2006 you give $25,000 to your 25-year-old daughter. The first $12,000 of your gift is not subject to the gift tax because of the annual exclusion. The remaining $13,000 is a taxable gift. As explained later under Applying the Unified Credit to Gift Tax, you may not have to pay the gift tax on the remaining $13,000. However, you do have to file a gift tax return.

Gift Splitting

If you or your spouse makes a gift to a third party, the gift can be considered as made one-half by you and one-half by your spouse. This is known as gift splitting. Both of you must agree to split the gift. If you do, you each can take the annual exclusion for your part of the gift. In 2006, gift splitting allowed married couples to give up to $24,000 to a person without making a taxable gift. If you split a gift you made, you must file a gift tax return to show that you and your spouse agree to use gift splitting. You must file a Form 709 even if half of the split gift is less than the annual exclusion.

· **Example**: Harold and his wife Helen agree to split the gifts they made during 2006. Harold gives his nephew George $21,000, and Helen gives her niece Gina $18,000. Although each gift is more than the annual exclusion ($12,000), by gift splitting they can make these gifts without making a taxable gift. Harold's gift to George is treated as one-half ($10,500) from Harold and one-half ($10,500) from Helen. Helen's gift to Gina is also treated as one-half ($9,000) from Helen and one-half ($9,000) from Harold. In each case, because one-half of the split gift is not more than the annual exclusion, it is not a taxable gift. However, each of them must file a gift tax return.

Applying the Unified Credit to Gift Tax

After you determine which of your gifts are taxable, you figure the amount of gift tax on the total taxable gifts and apply your unified credit for the year.

> **Example**: In 2006, you give your niece, Mary, a cash gift of $8,000. It is your only gift to her this year. You pay the $15,000 college tuition of your friend, David. You give your 25-year-old daughter Lisa $25,000. You also give your 27-year-old son Ken $25,000. Before 2006 you had never given a taxable gift. You apply the exceptions to the gift tax and the unified credit as follows:

1. Apply the educational exclusion. Payment of tuition expenses is not subject to the gift tax. Therefore, the gift to David is not a taxable gift.

2. Apply the annual exclusion. The first $12,000 you give someone during 2006 is not a taxable gift. Therefore, your $8,000 gift to Mary, the first $12,000 of your gift to Lisa, and the first $12,000 of your gift to Ken are not taxable gifts.

3. Apply the unified credit. The gift tax on $26,000 ($13,000 remaining from your gift to Lisa plus $13,000 remaining from your gift to Ken) is $5,120. You subtract the $5,120 from your unified credit of

$345,800 for 2006. The unified credit that you can use against the gift tax in a later year is $340,680. You do not have to pay any gift tax for 2006. However, you do have to file Form 709.

Filing a Gift Tax Return

You must file a gift tax return (Form 709) if any of the following apply:

1. You gave gifts to at least one person (other than your spouse) that are more than the annual exclusion for the year.

2. You and your spouse are splitting a gift.

3. You gave someone other than your spouse a gift of a future interest that he or she cannot possess, enjoy, or receive income from until sometime in the future.

4. You gave your spouse an interest in property that will be ended by a future event.

You do not have to file a gift tax return to report gifts to political organizations or gifts made by paying someone's tuition or medical expenses. You also do not need to report the following deductible gifts made to charities:

1. Your entire interest in property, if no other interest has been transferred for less than adequate consideration or for other than a charitable use.

2. A qualified conservation contribution that is a restriction (granted forever) on the use of real property.

Estate Tax

Estate tax may apply to your taxable estate at your death. Your taxable estate is your gross estate less allowable deductions.

Gross Estate

Your gross estate includes the value of all property in which you had an interest at the time of death. Your gross estate also will include the following:

- Life insurance proceeds payable to your estate or, if you owned the policy, to your heirs

- The value of certain annuities payable to your estate or your heirs

- The value of certain property you transferred within three years before your death

Taxable Estate

The allowable deductions used in determining your taxable estate include:

1. Funeral expenses paid out of your estate

2. Debts you owed at the time of death

3. The marital deduction (the value of the property that passes from your estate to your surviving spouse)

4. The charitable deduction (generally, the value of the property that passes from your estate to the United

States, any state, a political subdivision of a state, or to a qualifying charity for exclusively charitable purposes)

Applying the Unified Credit to Estate Tax

Any unified credit not used to eliminate gift tax can be used to eliminate or reduce estate tax.

Filing an Estate Tax Return

An estate tax return, Form 706, must be filed if the gross estate, plus any adjusted taxable gifts and specific gift tax exemption, is more than the filing requirement for the year of death. Adjusted taxable gifts is the total of the taxable gifts you made after 1976 that are not included in your gross estate. The specific gift tax exemption applies only to gifts made after September 8, 1976, and before 1977.

The following table lists the filing requirement for the estate of a decedent dying after 2001.

Year of Death	Filing Requirement
2006, 2007, and 2008	$2,000,000
2009	$3,500,000

Generation-Skipping Transfer Tax

The Generation-Skipping Transfer tax (GST) may apply to gifts or direct skips occurring at your death to skip persons. The GST tax is calculated on the value of the gift or bequest, after subtraction of any allocated GST exemption, at the maximum estate tax rate for the year involved. Each individual has a GST exemption equal to the applicable exclusion amount for the year. A direct skip is a transfer made during your life or occurring at your death that is:

1. Subject to the gift or estate tax

2. Of an interest in property

3. Made to a skip person

A "skip person" is a person who is assigned to a generation that is two or more generations below the generation assignment of the donor. For instance, your grandchild may be a skip person to you or your spouse. The GST tax is computed on the amount of the gift or bequest transferred to a skip person after subtraction of any GST exemption allocated to the gift or bequest at the maximum gift and estate tax rates.

4
Who Are the Parties to a Trust?

There are several parties to a trust, and each party has specific responsibilities to carry out as described below.

The Grantor

The grantor is the person who creates the trust. If you create a trust, you are the grantor. Other terms for grantor include "trustor" and "settlor."

The Initial Trustee

This is the person who manages the trust property. As long as he or she is alive, the grantor is also the trustee. The trustee's responsibilities include conferring property to the beneficiaries and taking care of other trust matters. If he or she wishes, a trustee can appoint a co-trustee to handle trust details. When the trust is a basic living one, the surviving spouse is the trustee. He or she has the responsibility of distributing the deceased's trust property and managing the ongoing revocable trust that holds his or her property. This includes trust property inherited from the deceased spouse.

In the case of an AB Trust, the surviving spouse uses the help of an expert to divide the property between Trust A (the trust of the deceased spouse) and Trust B (the trust of the surviving spouse). The surviving spouse can then distribute any gifts in the trust as bequeathed by the deceased spouse. The remaining trust property of the deceased is left in Trust A. As the trustee, the survivor is responsible for legally establishing and maintaining Trust A. This includes getting a federal taxpayer ID number and keeping trust records.

The Successor Trustee

This is the person who takes over after the initial trustee(s) dies or becomes incapacitated. A trust document is required to name a successor trustee. In the case of either a basic living trust or an AB Trust, the successor trustee possesses no authority while both trustees are alive and capable of managing their own affairs. The successor trustee has several responsibilities. He or she has to turn the property over to the beneficiaries as specified in the trust. In case of incapacitation of the trustees, he or she is required to manage the trust, prepare and file estate tax returns, and take care of any other specified responsibilities.

Naming a successor trustee is important. It should be someone who has your best interests, and those of the beneficiaries, at heart and who is trustworthy and willing to take on the task. A family member or trusted friend may be selected. Such a trustee should be competent in financial matters. He or she should know how to manage and invest your estate effectively. It is helpful for him or her to have the financial wherewithal to reimburse the trust in case he or she makes serious mistakes. The successor trustee often has the power (as permitted under state law) to buy and sell real estate, stocks and bonds, and other investments. It is important for this trustee to carry out the estate requirements in an honest and prudent manner. He or she is not allowed to profit or benefit personally ("self-dealing") from any transaction involving the estate. However, the successor trustee does have the authority to hire a professional to assist with management of the trust and to pay for expert advice with money from the trust.

If you wish, you can legally name more than one successor trustee. For example, you might want to name two or more of your children as co-successor trustees so as not to favor one over the other. However, it is important to make sure they all get along together; otherwise, the potential for conflict can hold up distribution of property or even result in lawsuits among the successor trustees. It may be best to name just one successor trustee.

A successor trustee is not paid for two reasons. First, distribution of property is not a difficult job. Second, the successor trustee can be a major beneficiary of the trust. There are two exceptions to the general rule of non-payment. If the grantor or grantors become incapacitated, then the successor trustee is entitled to reasonable compensation. The same is true of management of a child's trust. In either case, active management of the trusts is required, so payment is in order, especially if management lasts for years (as in the case of a child's trust.)

The Trust Beneficiaries

These are the individuals selected by the grantor to receive the trust property upon his or her death. You have the power to name anyone you want as a beneficiary. There are three kinds of beneficiaries in individual or basic shared trusts.

1. **Primary beneficiaries**. These are the individuals, groups, or institutions whom you select to receive specific property.

2. **Alternate or contingent beneficiaries**. These are beneficiaries you name to receive property left to a primary beneficiary if the primary beneficiary dies before you do.

3. **Remainder beneficiaries**. These are the beneficiaries who receive all trust assets not left to the first two types of beneficiaries.

In the case of an AB Trust, the types of beneficiaries are different. There is the life beneficiary — the surviving spouse — and the final beneficiaries. The final beneficiaries are named by each spouse for his or her trust property (Trust A or B).

The Trust Property

This includes any property specified in the trust. It is also called trust principal or trust estate. Property can include real estate, stocks, bonds, small business interests, art collections, and other valuables.

5
What Property Should Go Into a Trust?

When you create a trust, you must list each item of property to be held in trust. This list is called a schedule, and it is attached to the trust document. Only one schedule is required for an individual trust. For a basic shared trust there are three schedules:

- One for property owned solely by the wife

- One for property owned solely by the husband

- One for property owned jointly by the husband and wife

Any property you do not list does not go into the living trust, which means it is subject to probate. You must also prepare separate formal documents transferring property ownership to the trust and the trustee.

Properties to Include in Your Living Trust

List your most valuable property in the trust. This includes the following:

- Brokerage accounts (stocks, bonds, and other security accounts held by brokers)

- Business interests (including stock in closely-held corporations)

- Houses and other real estate

- Jewelry and antiques

- Money market accounts

- Royalties, patents, and copyrights

- Precious metals

- Valuable collections (stamps, coins, and other collectibles)

- Works of art

Properties Not to Include in Your Living Trust

If you have property of relatively little value, you do not need to place it in a living trust because it may be exempt from probate anyway. Do not include these types of property:

- **Annuities**: You name beneficiaries in the annuity policy's contract. This means they receive the money when you die outside of probate, so there is no need to put it in your living trust.

- **Automobiles**: The cars in your estate may not be that valuable. Also, insurance companies may be reluctant to insure a car owned by a trust. An exception might be a valuable car or collection of such cars. In that case, check with your insurance company to see if it insures cars owned by trusts. Many states' motor vehicle departments have forms that allow cars to be registered in joint tenancy. This allows you to avoid probate on vehicles.

- **Community Property With Right of Survivorship**: This law permits the half-interest in community property of one spouse to pass to the surviving spouse without the need to go through probate. As of this writing, only certain states allow this: Alaska, Arizona, California, Nevada, and Wisconsin.

- **Contaminated Property**: Federal law holds that responsible parties are liable for the costs of cleaning up contaminated land. These parties include past or current owners of the real estate, regardless of who contributed to the contamination. Such contamination includes toxic substances such as oil spills, dry cleaning solvents, and others. Cleanup can be a costly problem, so you do not want to leave it to the beneficiaries of your living trust.

- **Employee Stock Options**: The Internal Revenue Service's complicated rules can make transfer of stock options a dicey proposition, and it is best not to include these in your living trust. An exception is the transfer of stock options purchased on a recognized stock exchange. With stock options you have the right to buy a number of shares at a set price. This is a contractual right that can be transferred to your living trust. If you decide to take this route, be sure to hire the services of a lawyer who specializes in this complex area.

· **Income or Principal from Another Trust**: If you are entitled to leave interest or principal from another trust to your own beneficiaries, you are not allowed to do so through your living trust. This can only be done through your will.

· **IRAs, 401(k)s**: Such accounts or funds cannot be owned by a trust. However, you can still avoid probate on these accounts by directly naming a beneficiary to receive the monies when you die.

· **Joint Tenancy Property**: This property does not go through probate, so there is no need to transfer it into your living trust.

· **Life Insurance**: Your policy directly designates a beneficiary, so there is no need to put it in your trust.

· **Pay-on-Death Bank Accounts**: You name beneficiaries directly to receive funds from these accounts so they do not go through the probate process.

· **Personal Checking Accounts**: Do not include these in your trust unless you want to pay your bills in the name of the trust. People and institutions are not always familiar with trusts and may be suspicious of the fact that you are not writing checks in your own name.

- **Property You Buy or Sell Frequently**: This is particularly true if you do not expect to own the property when you die.

6
What Types of Trusts are There?

Trusts take a variety of forms because there are no standard forms they must take. However, there are basic trust classifications across all types.

One classification is whether a trust becomes effective during the grantor's lifetime or after the grantor's death. A living trust becomes effective during the grantor's lifetime. It is also called an inter-vivos trust, Latin for "during life."

Trusts can be created by two types of written instruments. These are:

- **Trust Agreement**. Used when the trust has a trustee other than the grantor. Both the grantor and the trustee are required to agree to the terms.

- **Declaration of Trust**. If the grantor is the sole trustee, the trust instrument is called a "declaration of trust." This is because the grantor is the only party to the trust.

A testamentary trust only becomes effective after the death of the testator. The trust is created under a Last Will and

Testament and because of this must also go through probate before it becomes effective.

Another basic classification of trusts is that of revocability or irrevocability. A revocable trust gives you the ability to change the terms of the trust as you see fit and is one of the benefits of a living trust. Unlike a will, it contains instructions for the long-term management of your assets during your lifetime, even in the event of disability. In a living trust, you can actually be the trustee, keeping full control over all property held in the trust. This property does not have to be scrutinized by a probate court before it reaches the people you want to inherit it, which can save time and expenses.

With an irrevocable trust, you cannot amend or revoke the trust once it is established. Normally, a gift of the property is made to the trust and is funded with after tax dollars. The trust is then established as a separate taxable entity and pays tax on its accumulated income. Trusts may receive a deduction for income distributed on a current basis. Although individuals may find an irrevocable trust of limited interest, this type of trust has its purpose. These are mainly in the area of tax avoidance and avoidance of probate fees. For example, an irrevocable trust is useful for life insurance planning. With a structured irrevocable trust, your beneficiaries can avoid fees and estate taxes on the insurance proceeds. Such a trust is also useful in providing your children with a fund for education or other planning purposes.

The Basic Living Trust for One Person (A Trust)

If you are single, a single parent, a widow, or the like, this trust allows you to leave part or all your property to specified beneficiaries (sister, brother, children). For example, if you own part of a home, you can leave your share to a sibling or your child or children. If you are a partner in a business or own shares in a corporation, you can transfer your shares into the trust if bylaws allow it. If the estate is less than one million dollars, there will be no probate fees or estate taxes. If it is worth more, then estate taxes will be due. The basic living trust also permits you to name your successor trustee(s) and leave property to minors or young adults through the Uniform Transfers to Minors Act (UMTA). (Chapter 8 includes extensive information on the UMTA.)

An example of a basic living trust for an individual is shown at the end of the chapter. First, here is an overview of the articles of the trust and a brief explanation of their purposes:

- **Article I: Declaration of Trust** — This section provides the name of the trust, the date on which it is executed, and designates the person(s) making the trust (the grantor and, in this case, the co-trustees).

- **Article II: Trust Property Disposition** — This article specifies transfer of the property to the trustees, how it shall be managed by the trustees, and who the beneficiaries of the trust are. All trust property should be listed in specific terms in an attached schedule.

- **Article III: Distributions to Beneficiaries Under Legal Age** — This article specifies how trust assets are to be managed by a trustee for beneficiaries who are under age. The trustee may be directed to use the assets for the support, welfare, and education of children.

- **Article IV: Right of Revocation and Amendment** — This article establishes your right to revoke and amend the trust in any way you desire.

- **Article V: Designation of Successor Trustees** — Within this article, you name successor trustees who will manage the trust in the event the trustees die, become incapacitated, resign, or for any reason cannot fulfill their duties.

- **Notary's Acknowledgement** — The Notary Public's signature establishes the trust as a legal and binding document.

This is a simple living trust that includes the basic elements — whose trust it is, what the assets are, who will manage the trust, and who gets the trust assets. More complicated trusts will include additional articles such as general administrative provisions, child's trusts, custodianships, and other specifics. It all depends on your needs and the complexities of your particular situation. A basic living trust form that you can adapt for your own needs is in the Appendix.

Married or unmarried couples can also use such a trust if their estates are valued below one million dollars. The surviving spouse will receive the entire estate because there will be no probate fees and no estate taxes since the estate is small. However, a couple should consider an AB trust first (described below) because of its advantages.

The AB Trust

This is a standard planning tool for married couples. It is an effective means of avoiding estate taxes if you have a large enough estate. When you establish an AB trust, your purpose is to keep the estate of the deceased spouse legally separate from the estate of the surviving spouse. This is done to insure the surviving spouse will benefit from the decedent's property.

If, for example, you establish the trust as the husband, your trust will be Trust A and that of your wife will be Trust B. If you die first, your wife then receives all income from your trust property and can use the trust's principle to meet basic needs. The reverse is also true, of course. An AB trust maximizes the personal estate tax exemption by having each spouse take full advantage of it.

Here is an example of how an AB trust can work. Assume you are a married couple, and you are the wife. You and your husband own $2 million together. If you each left your $1 million to the other, the surviving spouse would own $2 million. Of that amount, $500,000 would be taxable if that spouse died in 2008. To avoid the hefty taxes on that amount, you create an AB trust. You each leave $1 million in your respective trust (A and B) and name your children as beneficiaries. If you die, your $1 million goes into your husband's trust, but because the amount of the trust is less than the federal estate tax exemption ($2 million for 2008), no tax is due.

This form of trust does have its disadvantages. An important disadvantage is that the surviving spouse cannot sell his or her spouse's share of the trust property held in Trust A because it must be made available for the final beneficiaries. The surviving spouse is entitled to income generated by Trust A, however, and to certain allowances for his or her health and support. Another disadvantage is the administrative costs of maintaining an AB living trust. If you are the surviving spouse, you must keep separate books and records for Trust A and Trust B to make proper and effective use of the trust assets.

There is also the necessity of trust tax returns. The surviving spouse bears the burden of filing an obligatory annual trust income tax return and must get a taxpayer ID number for the marital life estate trust. In addition, there is uncertainty about the tax laws since Congress is involved in this area. Congress may change estate tax laws. Depending on estate tax legislation, you may need to change or revoke a living trust in the future. Finally, there is the matter of attorney and accountant fees. The surviving spouse will want to select the most tax-efficient way to divide the couple's assets between the trusts, and that may require the services of a lawyer or accountant.

An AB trust may not be needed or wanted by some couples. One instance is when one spouse is much younger than the other. Because the younger spouse will likely live a long time, it may not be necessary to place the burden of the estate-tax-saving living trust on that spouse. Another instance is that of younger couples. They may opt for a basic probate-avoidance living trust and then, revoke that trust later in life to replace it with an AB trust. Plus, if one spouse unexpectedly dies, the survivor inherits everything free of estate tax anyway. That spouse will then have ample time to use the money and find another way to save on estate taxes.

The last instance is that of couples with children from prior marriages. There is the possibility that conflict will erupt between the surviving spouse (who may need use of the assets) and the final beneficiaries (who want to save all assets for themselves) about how the trust should be used. The beneficiaries need to understand that an AB trust's purpose is to ensure their final inheritance will be secure and safe from estate tax. See the Appendix for an example of an AB trust.

The AB Disclaimer Trust

One way of overcoming the main disadvantage of the AB trust (inability to sell the spouse's share of Trust A property) is to use a disclaimer. A disclaimer is a written declaration by the beneficiary that he or she declines to accept property left to him or her. All beneficiaries possess the legal right to disclaim property bequeathed to them. They cannot be compelled to accept an inheritance. An AB Disclaimer Trust does not force the estate to be split. Instead, each spouse makes a complete gift of his or her estate to the other spouse. Then, when one spouse dies, the surviving spouse has the option of deciding whether he or she wants to fund the disclaimer trust to potentially save on federal estate taxes. The strategy is to choose a year in which the estate tax is less or non-existent to fund the trust. Here is an example of how an AB disclaimer trust works:

> Ted and Tina jointly own property worth around $2.5 million. They prepare an AB trust. Being cautious, they assume that both of them could die during 2007. If that event occurs, their combined estate would be $500,000 over the 2007 threshold of $2 million. Therefore, they want to establish A and B trusts to make sure no estate taxes would be levied upon the death of the second spouse. Of course the likelihood of both of them dying in 2007

is statistically small, and if both of them survive beyond 2007 (and assuming the estate does not grow dramatically), there is no need to establish Trust A before 2011 (when the estate tax exemption is currently set to roll back to $1 million). Ted and Tina could leave their property to each other. The survivor's estate of $2.5 million would remain below the estate tax threshold so there would be no tax benefit from having a Trust A. Given this situation, here is how the disclaimer declaration works: If Ted dies in 2009 when the exemption is $3.5 million and the estate has grown to potentially $3 million, its value still remains under the estate tax threshold. Tina can now decide to inherit all of Ted's property and not disclaim any of it. There is no creation of a Trust A.

There are disadvantages with a disclaimer trust. For one thing, it gives the surviving spouse total control over trust assets left to him or her. That means he or she can choose to inherit the deceased spouse's property right away, even though that may not be the best choice for tax purposes. Another disadvantage is the need to keep up with the changing tax laws regarding trusts. See the Appendix for an example of an AB Disclaimer trust.

ABC Trusts

These trusts are also called Qualified Terminal Interest Property trusts (QTIP). ABC trusts may be used when a husband or wife wishes to leave a surviving spouse the income from a trust during the surviving spouse's lifetime and to bequeath the remainder to their children upon the surviving spouses' death. Here is an example of such a trust:

> Assume Jeff has two children from a prior marriage. He is concerned his current wife Mary will not provide for those children. Jeff wants to provide for his ex-wife Sarah and for the children from his prior marriage. To accomplish this objective, Jeff creates and sets up an ABC trust and funds it with stock worth $3.5 million dollars. The result is that the trust provides Sarah with the income from the trust during her lifetime. When Mary dies, his children are provided with equal shares in the stock used to fund the trust.

Estate taxes are applied when the beneficiaries receive the trust assets. If a spouse is over the current exemption limit and he or she lives long enough, the increasing exemption will reduce or even eliminate the federal estate tax hit. A potential disadvantage of the ABC or QTIP trust is your children will not see any of the money in the trust until your spouse dies. See the Appendix for an example of an ABC trust.

The Credit Shelter Trust

This type of trust is also called a "bypass trust," an "exemption trust," or a "family trust," and is a useful method of avoiding probate and saving on estate taxes for wealthy couples. It is designed for couples who have a combined income over the estate tax threshold and who want to leave their property to each other. At present, the estate tax affects only people who die leaving a taxable estate of more than $2 million. It minimizes taxes by applying the federal personal estate tax exemption to both spouses. The personal estate exemption allows a set amount of property to pass free of federal tax. The amount depends on the year of death. The exemption is applied by keeping the estate of the deceased spouse legally separate from the estate of the surviving spouse, while allowing the survivor to benefit from the deceased's property. Here is an example based on the $2.5 million exemption amount allowed in 2007:

> Assume John fails to establish a credit shelter trust and leaves his entire $5 million estate outright to his wife Jane. After John's death, his estate incurs no federal estate taxes due to the marital deduction. Upon Jane's death in 2007, only half of the estate is exempt — $2.5 million. Their children will have to cough up about $1,125,000 of federal estate taxes on the other half. Obviously, this is a situation to be avoided.

> If John had established a credit shelter trust, he would have willed only $2.5 million to Jane outright and put the other $2.5 million in the credit shelter trust. Jane would be entitled to income from the trust after his death. After the death of Jane the assets in the trust will not be part of her estate, and they pass tax-free to their children. The other $2.5 million is also untaxed due to Jane's own $2.5 million exemption. Their children inherit $5 million free of estate tax (assuming no appreciation or depreciation of the value of the assets) — a savings in taxes.

A final advantage of the family trust is that it permits sprinkling. This term refers to the practice of allocating income and principal to those family members who need it, such as children. The funds can then remain intact until all educational, medical, and other needs can be met. It allows the trustee to decide how to spread the money among several beneficiaries and may create a more fair distribution of assets.

The Testamentary Trust

This is a trust set forth in your will which becomes effective after your death. The assets in a testamentary trust must still pass through probate. However, it can still save you a considerable amount in estate taxes. It is a good method of providing for young children and any others who will need management of their assets after your death.

In establishing a trust, choose one that best fits your situation. For example, if you are single, use an A Trust for an individual. With this trust, you can leave all or part of your property to the beneficiaries. You can also name your successor trustee(s) and leave property to minors or young adults through a child's trust or under the UTMA.

If you are married, use a form of AB Trust depending on your financial situation. With this trust, you and your spouse are co-trustees. You and your spouse both retain control over your respective separate properties, entitling either of you to sell your property, give it away, or leave it in the trust. Each of you can also name beneficiaries to inherit the property. In addition, you have the option of amending the trust to name different or more beneficiaries for your properties. You also have the ability to add separately-owned property to the trust later.

U.S. trust law is set up to favor traditional, married couples. This means non-traditional couples face obstacles. For example, a non-traditional surviving partner may be discover upon his or her partner's death that he or she has no rights to the assets of the deceased partner and could be forced to move from a residence they shared. Moreover, if children are involved, it is possible the surviving partner could lose guardianship of the children if the surviving partner did not adopt the children prior to their partner's incapacity or death.

A living trust can eliminate or alleviate problems faced by non-traditional couples. First, living trusts are not as contestable as wills. That means there is less opportunity for confrontation from family members who might want to challenge a non-traditional couple's relationship. Second, a living trust offers more privacy compared to the process of public probate, which may be as valuable to the non-traditional couple as the finances involved.

For conventional unmarried couples, the conventional Unmarried AB trust may be a good choice for those who jointly own the couple's primary assets. In addition to this trust, each partner may specify assets not jointly owned (owned by only one person) through a separate property agreement. An Unmarried AB trust is similar to a Married AB Trust, but it has been written to address the limitations on rights that face non-traditional couples.

A Partner A-A trust is suitable for two persons of the same gender. It is similar to two single trusts blended together in which the couple's assets are all separately owned by one partner or the other.

In either case, the trusts can be revocable or irrevocable. If a trust is revocable and the relationship ends, the trust can be revoked and assets returned to each individual, or other suitable arrangements can be made. For example, an arrangement can be made on how to handle the split in the value of a residence in which one partner wishes to continue to live. This avoids the problem with joint ownership and rights of survivorship (common among non-traditional couples), where splitting up can require one partner to seek court approval to partition the joint ownership title and force the sale of the property.

It is also critical for non-traditional couples to have two vital documents drawn up — the Durable Power of Attorney for Health Care and the Advanced Health Care Directive. These documents are important because state authorities, hospitals, or even family members may not recognize the partner's participation regarding health care decisions that affect a hospitalized partner. See the Appendix for examples of these documents combined into one form.

Other Type of Trusts

The trusts described below are more complex, and you may not have a need for them. However, this section will familiarize you with the purpose of each type in case you have such a need in the future.

Asset Protection Trusts (Self-Settled Spendthrift Trusts)

As the name indicates, these trusts are designed to protect your assets from creditors. They are irrevocable living trusts. They can be off-shore (Foreign Asset Protection Trust, or FAPT) or on-shore (Domestic Asset Protection Trust, or DAPT). They are also referred to as Alaska, Nevada, or Delaware trusts, after the states that have anti-creditor trust acts. This form of trust has three advantages:

1. It protects you against creditors. (This varies from one state to another)

2. It has a shorter time (statute of limitations) in which a creditor can challenge a transfer to the trust.

3. The trust makes it more difficult for a creditor to prove that a transfer into the trust was a fraudulent one.

If this type of trust sounds too good to be true, you are right. Federal and state governments regard them with suspicion and tend to view them as loopholes, particularly for corporate officers, and have tightened the rules (search the Internet for more information on The Sarbanes-Oxley Act of 2002 and The 2005 Bankruptcy Reform Act). Historically, bankruptcy courts also have little respect for them. You will want to tread carefully in this area if you are considering one of these trusts.

Charitable Trusts

A charitable trust is one that has one or more charitable beneficiaries. It has to be properly established under federal tax laws. If you are the grantor of such a trust, you will be entitled to deduct a portion of the amount contributed to the charitable trust as a current charitable income tax deduction. Charitable trusts come in several different forms.

Charitable Split-Interest Trusts

Charitable "split-interest" trusts have both charitable and non-charitable beneficiaries. They are called split-interest because the interest of the charitable beneficiaries is separate from the interest of the non-charitable beneficiaries. There are several different kinds of split-interest trusts, and each type has a name that indicates the nature of the split interest.

Charitable Lead Trusts

If you possess a large estate and are looking for a method to pass more on to your heirs, a form of charitable lead trust may be a good choice. It is a plan that allows you to transfer assets to future generations at a significantly reduced estate tax or gift cost. You can create a charitable trust under a living trust or a testamentary trust, but if any distributions are to be made during the grantor's lifetime, then such a trust must be an irrevocable living trust.

A charitable lead trust is called a "non-grantor" trust. It is called a non-grantor trust because the assets ultimately revert to non-charitable beneficiaries other than the grantor. "Lead" is the term used because the trust leads with a stream of income to charity before the assets regress to the leftover beneficiaries. It is also called an "annuity" trust because it provides fixed annual payments to charity during the term of the trust. Tax benefits will vary according to the type of charitable trust established.

These trusts provide payments to one or more charities for a fixed number of years. The present interest goes to one or more charities and is called the "lead" interest, thus the term "lead trust." When charitable interest ends, the remainder of the trust assets goes to non-charitable beneficiaries and is called the "remainder interest." This is an example of a "split-interest trust," as described above.

The Internal Revenue Service strictly regulates these trusts. These trusts must comply with federal tax laws to receive tax deductions for charitable contributions and gain favorable tax treatment. These trusts are complex, but a simple example will give you an idea of how they work: Assume Jennifer Smith establishes a charitable lead trust and places $20,000 in it. The trust instrument stipulates that 10 percent of the value of the trust is to be given to XYZ Association each year for ten years. After that time has passed, the trust terminates. The trust assets (the remainder interest) pass to Jennifer's living children.

Charitable Remainder Trusts

These trusts provide for payments of income or principal to one or more non-charitable beneficiaries for a fixed number of years or for life (lead interest). At the end of the lead interest, the remainder of the trust assets passes to one or more qualified charities (remainder interest). This is another example of a split-interest trust. The present interest (lead interest) goes to non-charities, and the remainder interest goes to charities. These trusts must also meet federal tax laws to receive favorable tax treatment; in this case, it is for both income tax and estate tax deductions for charitable contributions. Here is a basic example to illustrate how these complex trusts operate: Let us assume Jennifer decides to establish a charitable remainder trust. She gives $20,000 to a charitable remainder trust she has established. The trust instrument stipulates that 10 percent of the value of the trust is to be given to Jennifer's daughter Laura during Laura's lifetime. Upon Laura's death, the trust will end, and all trust assets (the remainder interest) pass to the XYZ Association.

Charitable Remainder Annuity Trusts (CRAT)

Charitable Remainder Annuity Trusts are trusts that pay a fixed dollar amount each year to the non-charitable (lead interest) beneficiaries. Here is an example of how a CRAT works:

> Assume you are John Smith, who owns securities that cost you $60,000 and have now appreciated to $100,000 in value. You donate these securities to a university or charity to establish a charitable remainder annuity trust. Your wife Amy is age 65, and you name her as the lifetime beneficiary. The CRAT trust agreement provides for annual payments to Amy of $6,000, or 6 percent of the initial trust principal for life. In this situation, you qualify for a $49,744 income tax deduction. Beyond that, you may avoid the tax on the $40,000 appreciation that would have resulted had you sold the securities. Upon your death, the trust principal will pass to the university or charity for a purpose designated by you.

A CRAT has several advantages:

- The annuity trust can be paid to you and your other beneficiaries for lifetime or for a term of up to 20 years.

·   If you fund your CRAT with appreciated property, no up-front capital gains tax is payable. This means you can contribute appreciated but low-yielding assets to the trust and put the whole value of your gift to work producing higher income for you.

·   Beyond avoidance of the capital gains tax, you also receive a charitable income tax deduction when you create an annuity trust. That deduction will be based on the full fair market value of the assets you contributed, reduced by the present value of the income interest you kept.

·   When your annuity trust ends (upon the death of the last beneficiary or at the end of the trust term), the remaining balance is then available for the use you chose when you created the trust.

Potential disadvantages of a CRAT are that the trust income may vary, and it may require a minimum gift amount to be created.

Charitable Remainder Unitrusts (CRUT)

Charitable Remainder Unitrusts are charitable remainder trusts that pay a fixed percentage of the value of the trust each year to the non-charitable (lead interest) beneficiaries.

The charitable remainder unitrust is revalued every year and then pays you a fixed percentage of the fair market value of the trust assets. Similar to the annuity trust, you are allowed to claim a charitable deduction on your income taxes the year the trust was created. The received payments will be taxed as ordinary income, or in certain circumstances as capital gain or tax-free return of principal. Here is an example of such a trust:

> Assume you transfer $100,000 to create an irrevocable charitable remainder unitrust that will provide you with life income payments. The trust agreement is set up so that you receive 6 percent of the fair market value of the assets on an annual basis. The first year you receive $6,000 (100,000 x 6%). A year later, the trust assets are now valued at $120,000, so you are paid $7,200 ($120,000 x 6%). If the trust assets are worth $110,000 at the start of the next year, you will receive $6,600 ($110,000 x 6%), and the same formula would continue to be used for each of the following years. If trust income is more than the stated payout percentage, the excess is added to your unitrust assets and reinvested.

In addition to the advantages mentioned above, you can receive increased income for life and support multiple charitable causes while doing it. Disadvantages include variance of income and the possibility of a minimum gift amount to establish the trust.

Net Income with Make Up Charitable Remainder Unitrusts Provisions (NIMCRUT)

These are a type of charitable remainder unitrust that provides a net income make up provision. They stipulate an annual distribution of income to the non-charitable beneficiaries equal to a fixed percentage of the trust fund. However, the trust payout is limited to the net income if the net income of the trust is less than the fixed payout percentage. This is the "make up" provision of such trusts; it allows the trust to compensate for any deficiencies during those years in which the net income of the trust exceeds the fixed payout percentage. Here is an example of how a NIMCRUT works:

> Assume Jennifer establishes such a trust and stipulates that it is required to pay 5 percent of the value of the trust fund each year. In the first year, the trust has net income equal to 3 percent of the value of the trust fund. This means that distribution to non-charitable beneficiaries during that year is limited to 3 percent. However, in the second year, the charitable remainder unitrust's net income increased to 9 percent of the value of the trust fund. Therefore, in that year, the trust can pay 5 percent (the normal payout) to the non-income beneficiaries, but it can also pay an additional 2 percent to the non-charitable beneficiaries. This is to "make up" for the deficiency in the first year. A NIMCRUT provides flexibility to adapt to changing conditions and ensures the non-charitable beneficiaries receive a constant amount.

Constructive Trusts

These trusts are created by a court in situations where no formal trust actually exists or when misconduct is committed (for example, by a trustee). In the latter case, a constructive trust is used as a remedial device to compel the defendant to convey title to the property to the plaintiff. Such trusts may involve a passive and temporary arrangement in which the trustee's only duty is to transfer the title and possession to the beneficiary. Therefore, a constructive trust is not a trust in the classic sense in which the trustee has administration duties over a number of years.

Crummey Trusts

A Crummey Trust is named after D. Clifford Crummey. Such an instrument is a life insurance trust with certain provisions that allow gifts to the trust to qualify for the annual gift tax exclusion. At the time the trust was established in the 1960s, the IRS annual gift tax exclusion only applied to gifts of present interest, not future interest — when the insured died and the death proceeds were paid into the trust. To avoid this problem, Crummey created a life insurance trust with a stipulation that prohibited the trustee from using any money gifted to the trust for at least 30 to 60 days after the gift was made. During that period, the beneficiaries had the right to withdraw the money if they desired to do so. If they did not withdraw the money during the 30 to 60 day period, then their withdrawal rights ended and the money could be used to pay any premiums due. Of course the grantor never intended to have any of the money withdrawn from the trust during that one- to two-month period. The right was given to the beneficiaries only to qualify the gift for the annual gift tax exclusion.

The IRS claimed the provision was a sham and went to court, but the IRS lost. The court ruled that regardless of whether the beneficiaries actually withdrew the money or not, they had the right to do so. That right was all that was needed to give the beneficiaries a present interest in the gift. The name Crummey trust is given to an irrevocable life insurance trust that gives the beneficiaries the right to withdraw a gift for a set time to qualify it for the annual gift tax exclusion.

Dynasty Trusts

This type of trust has its roots in the early 1900s in the United States. At that time, several powerful and influential industrialists and entrepreneurs had amassed tremendous fortunes, including oil mogul John D. Rockefeller, Henry Ford, and steel magnate Andrew Carnegie. They wanted to preserve their estates and avoid taxation. They did not want tax burdens to fall on their children or their grandchildren. With their money, they were able to tap into the expertise of the top tax professionals. The result was the creation of the dynasty trust.

These trusts are designed to last beyond the time permitted by the "rule against perpetuities." This is a complex legal doctrine that limits the amount of time property can be controlled after death by a person's instructions in a will. The idea is that a person could leave property to heirs ad infinitum. Thus the rule is designed to prevent property from being held in perpetual trust and in perpetual avoidance of taxes. The rule refers to the lifetime of any beneficiary living at the time of the creation of the trust plus 21 years. However, the rule varies from state to state.

A dynasty trust is designed to get around this rule. In effect, it may be set up to last forever, ensuring generation after generation receives trust distributions. Dynasty trusts may be created as revocable, irrevocable, or testamentary trusts.

As of this writing, dynasty trusts are available in all 50 states. However, laws may subject these trusts to the "rule against perpetuities" mentioned above. This rule forces trusts to end roughly between 80 to 110 years after they are created. At this writing, there are statutes in 20 states revoking this rule. These include Arizona, Colorado, Delaware, Florida, Illinois, Missouri, Ohio, Washington, and Wisconsin, as well as the District of Columbia. Individuals throughout the United States can establish and maintain trusts in these states that can continue until all the trust's funds have been distributed or until the last living descendant of the creator of the trust dies.

Generation Skipping Trusts

A generation skipping trust is designed to save on estate taxes. This is done by preserving the trust principle for the grandchildren while the children receive only income. This creates a situation in which the children never legally own the property; therefore, it is not subject to estate tax upon their death. Such trusts can be created as a revocable, irrevocable, or testamentary trust.

Grantor Retained Income Trusts (GRIT)

These are trusts in which the grantor transfers property in trust but keeps the right to receive the trust income for life or for a specified term. The objective of a GRIT trust is to reduce the valuation of property for federal tax purposes upon the grantor's death. There are three types in use today:

- Grantor Retained Annuity Trust (GRAT)

· Grantor Retained Income Trust (GRIT)

· Qualified Personal Residence Trust (QPRT)

In each of these trusts, the federal estate tax laws require only that the income interest retained by the grantor be included in the grantor's estate upon his or her death for federal estate tax purposes. This commonly represents a significant discount from the full value of the property. GRITs, GRATs, and QPRTs are irrevocable trusts and are therefore regulated by federal income tax laws.

Grantor Retained Annuity Trust (GRAT)

A GRAT is funded with a single contribution of assets, the trust pays a percentage of the initial contribution, either fixed or with a predetermined increase (the annuity), to the donor for a term of years. The trust distributes the remaining assets to other beneficiaries, and not the donor, at the end of the term. The purpose of the GRAT is to shift future appreciation on the GRAT assets to other beneficiaries at a minimal gift tax cost. The assets transferred to the GRAT must appreciate at a higher rate than the IRS's assumed rate of return for the strategy to be effective. When this occurs, the difference between the actual rate of return on the investment and the IRS's assumed rate of return passes to the beneficiaries at the end of the GRAT term free of gift tax. The donor transfers assets to and from the trust and keeps the right to receive an annuity for a specified time. After that time, the remaining trust assets pass either outright or in trust to the donor's beneficiaries. Under GRAT terms, the donor has the right to receive an amount equal to the value transferred to the GRAT plus interest. The remainder beneficiaries then receive everything in excess of that value.

Here is an illustration of how a GRAT works:

> Assume you are 62 years old and you put $500,000 in a grantor retained annuity trust with a term of ten years. You have a 6.5 percent retained annuity interest ($32,500 per year). During the term of the trust, the taxable gift (subject to the year in which trust was formed) will be only $242,333.50 because the children will not get the trust property for ten years. Therefore, you will be able to remove $500,000 (or more if the trust property averages more than a 6.5 percent return) from your estate by making a taxable gift of only $242,333.

Of course it is possible that the trust assets will not appreciate as expected. If, for example, the GRAT only has a rate of return of 3 percent, you will receive back all the trust assets through the annuity payments, and nothing will be left for the benefit of the remainder beneficiaries. However, you will not have wasted an appreciable amount of the exemption from federal gift tax. When a GRAT works, it works well; when it does not, then your loss is minimal. Therefore, such a trust is a vehicle for holding a highly speculative investment that has the potential for significant appreciation — or deprecation. It can be used to hold equity investments that have lower risk, but still have potential for significant appreciation. Here are other GRAT tax considerations to consider:

- The advantages of the GRAT strategy are lost if the donor dies before the end of the annuity period because the trust assets will then be included in the donor's estate. This means you should use of a relatively short annuity period. Also, it may be easier to exceed the IRS rate of return over a short period than a long period. For example, an annualized rate of return of 20 percent on an investment over a two-year period occurs more often than a 20 percent annualized rate of return on an investment over a ten-year period. The Internal Revenue Service has recognized this, and it has become sensitive to the use of short-term GRATs. A two-year annuity term is considered an aggressive strategy while a four- or five-year term is considered less aggressive.

· A GRAT should be taxed as a grantor trust for income tax purposes. One benefit of this tax is the donor can report the GRAT income (during the annuity period) on his or her individual income tax return and pay the resulting taxes from the his or her funds. If the pre-tax return on its assets exceeds the IRS assumed rate, the GRAT strategy will produce gifts to the ultimate beneficiaries. Another benefit is the GRAT can pay the annuity to the donor by using appreciated property without the distribution being treated as a taxable sale of the property.

· There is no limit on the number of GRATs a person can create. Therefore, it is better to have multiple GRATs (each holding a different investment) than a single GRAT with a diversified portfolio. This prevents investments that do not appreciate substantially from diminishing the overall return of the GRAT.

Grantor Retained Income Trust (GRIT)

A Grantor Retained Income Trust (GRIT) is also a vehicle for reducing gift taxes on the transfer of assets to the next generation. As with GRATs, it works well with highly appreciating assets, including closely held stock. Because the value of the gift is determined on funding of the trust, any appreciation of the assets passes gift tax free to the remainder beneficiaries. The funding of the GRIT is a taxable gift by the settlor to the remainder beneficiaries. The gift amount is determined by reference to Internal Revenue Service actuarial tables, which move up and down monthly depending upon the current federal interest rates. GRITs have several advantages:

- To avoid the gift tax, asset appreciation is moved out of the estate.

- The settlor keeps some or all the income from the transferred assets for the duration of the GRIT.

- The transfer costs (such as gift tax) are lowered because a taxable gift is made only so that the value of the assets at the time of the transfer exceeds the actuarial value of the retained income interest.

- The assets funding the trust are not taxed in the settlor's estate upon his or her subsequent death for as long as the settlor survives the GRIT term.

- The settlor is able to maintain control of the assets for a longer period than possible with a direct gift.

Of course there are potential disadvantages to GRITs. If the settlor dies during the trust term, the trust assets may be included in the settlor's estate. If this occurs, then none of the benefits are gained while incurring the transaction costs. This means the trust term must be carefully chosen so that the settler will outlive that term. Otherwise, the settlor loses the economic benefit of the assets during his or her remaining lifetime.

Qualified Personal Residence Trusts (QPRT)

If you are interested in reducing the value of your personal residence upon your death for federal estate tax purposes, QPRTs will allow you to transfer your home to an irrevocable living trust while you still live in the home. This will reduce the home's value for federal estate tax purposes. To establish the trust, you must first execute the trust document. The second step is to deed your residence to the QPRT. Next, within the trust document, you state a set time during which the trust holds title to your residence before it would transfer the title to the beneficiaries. Fourth, during the trust term, you treat your home no differently than you do now; you continue to maintain the home. Finally, after the trust term you could remain in the home by renting it from the beneficiaries.

QPRTs have the following advantages:

> · Your residence is transferred out of your estate at a reduced tax value. The amount of your tax free transfer amount you would have to "spend" to move your residence out of your estate would be less than the actual value of the residence. This benefit occurs because the tax regulations state that the value of the residence deeded to the trust is reduced by the value

of your use of the residence during the specific time the trust holds the residence.

- As of the day it is deeded to the trust, your residence is transferred out of your estate. This has the effect of saving the estate tax that would have been paid at your death on the increased value (appreciation) of the residence during your lifetime.

There are also non-tax advantages. Since a QPRT accomplishes the transfer of your residence during your lifetime, the act reduces the expense and administrative details required of your family upon your death. In addition, since you are present to oversee the transfer, your intentions are clear. This has the potential to reduce or eliminate any prospective acrimony among your beneficiaries. Also, since you no longer "own" your home, it should receive asset protection if you later run into financial or legal problems.

There are also potential disadvantages with QPRTs:

- After the expiration of the set time in the QPRT, you no longer have the title to the property; it has been transferred to your beneficiaries. Depending on the family situation, this could be problematic if there is conflict with the beneficiaries. However, this problem can be headed off by signing a lease contract with the beneficiaries at the same time as the QRPT is executed. The lease would stipulate that you have the right to rent your residence from them at a fair rental rate after the QPRT time period has expired. This arrangement has an additional benefit; it transfers the rental money out of your estate with no transfer tax and no reduction in your annual federal exclusion per donee.

· Since your residence is passed to your beneficiaries without being exposed to estate tax, the income tax basis carries over to your trust beneficiaries, and is not stepped-up to fair market value at death. Therefore, if the home is later sold, it is likely that a capital gains tax will be owed unless a beneficiary first acquires title from the other beneficiaries and then converts the home into his or her own personal residence. If that is done, then the personal residence exclusion may offset any gain. This action saves substantially on taxes even if the capital gains tax must be paid because it may be less than one-half of the estate tax.

Life Insurance Trusts

These are irrevocable trusts and are designed to hold life insurance on the life of the grantor or another person. Their goal is to exclude the life insurance proceeds payable on the death of the grantor from federal estate taxation. The grantor can designate beneficiaries to receive the policy's death benefits upon his or her death. For federal estate tax purposes, the death benefits must be included in the grantor's estate if he or she owns a life insurance policy. Individuals and couples with large estates find life insurance trusts attractive in terms of dealing with federal estate taxes. When life insurance is used to pay estate taxes, the heirs get the full benefit of the estate assets they inherited. This results in life insurance trusts being one of the most popular trusts around (after bypass trusts). Whole life insurance may be used to pay estate taxes. In the case of a single individual, the insurance is written on the life of that person. When he or she dies, the proceeds from the insurance are then used to pay the federal estate taxes. The heirs then get the complete value of the estate assets. In the case of a married couple, the partners may buy joint and survivorship (second-to-die) life insurance. In the case of survivorship insurance, the proceeds are only payable upon the death of the second spouse.

A potential disadvantage of life insurance trusts is they are sensitive to changes in the estate tax laws. Another is they are irrevocable; once formed, the terms cannot be changed. Costs of setting up a life insurance trust can also be a disadvantage, but they pale in comparison to the tax-saving benefits. There is another disadvantage that can be avoided by having the trustee apply for the life insurance policy on creation of the trust. The reason for doing this is because if you, for example, obtain the policy and then transfer it to the trustee, the policy proceeds will be included in the insured's gross estate if you do not survive the transfer by at least three years. By having the trustee obtain the policy, you keep the value of trust assets lower.

Pet Trusts

A pet trust is a legal instrument that ensures your pet receives proper care after your death or in the event of your disability. As settlor of the trust, you choose a trustee to provide proper care for the pet according to your instructions. In addition to naming a trustee, your pet trust can name a pet caretaker, the person who will actually take possession of the pet. That person will then use the specified trust money to pay for your pet's care and expenses. The trustee and caretaker can be the same person. To ensure proper care of the pet, you should name alternate caretakers in the event your first choice is unwilling or unable to serve as your pet's caretaker. If you are fearful your pet might end up without a home, you might want to consider naming an animal sanctuary or no-kill shelter as caretakers.

In terms of money to provide for the pet's care, consider the following factors: the type of animal, its life expectancy, desired standard of living for the animal, potential medical treatment costs, and payment of the trustee for his or her services. Do not forget to earmark money for animal care when the caretaker is out of town, on vacation, ill, or otherwise temporarily unavailable or unable to provide personal care for the animal.

You may want to avoid placing an excessively large amount of money in the pet trust for the simple reason that it can lead to a contest of the trust by disgruntled heirs and/or beneficiaries. In this case, a court may find that the bequest was out of line with the needs of the pet and reduce the amount. To ensure the best quality of life for the pet, include specific instructions for trustee and caretaker — diet, daily routine, toys, crates, grooming, socialization, preferred veterinarian, caretaker compensation, and other expenses.

Resulting Trusts

This is a type of implied trust. It is created through operation of law and occurs in situations in which the actions of the parties involved and the nature of the transaction imply an intention to create a trust. Such a trust may occur when someone fails to give up his or her beneficial interest in property, either intentionally or by accident.

Special Needs Trusts

These trusts are established for beneficiaries who are developmentally disabled or mentally ill and lack the mental capacity to handle their financial affairs. Special needs trusts are designed to ensure these individuals can enjoy the use of property intended to be held for their benefit. In addition, they are created to prevent beneficiaries from losing access to essential government benefits and services. When a person receives government benefits, an inheritance, a gift, or money for damages in a personal injury law suit those funds can reduce or eliminate the person's eligibility for such benefits. A special needs trust avoids this problem. Such trusts may include a provision that terminates the trust if it makes the beneficiary ineligible for government benefits. These trusts can be created as a revocable or irrevocable living trust or testamentary trust.

Spendthrift Trusts

A spendthrift trust is designed to prevent the beneficiary or beneficiaries from wasting their money or to prevent money going to a creditor. This kind of trust may give the trustee a wide range in terms of disbursements.

A spendthrift trust may be a revocable or irrevocable living trust or a testamentary trust. However, for maximum effectiveness, such trusts should be irrevocable.

Totten Trusts

This is an "informal" trust. Not a trust in the true sense, it is created during the grantor's lifetime by depositing money into a bank or financial institution account. The deposit is made in the grantor's name as the trustee for another person, who is named as the beneficiary. When the grantor dies, the account is transferred to the beneficiary, but it is taxed as part of the grantor's estate. Money deposited into an account is not considered a completed gift until the grantor's death or until the happening of another event that unambiguously reflects the gift during the grantor's lifetime. If the account is jointly owned, the regulations covering joint accounts apply. When all account owners die, the beneficiary becomes the lawful owner.

Banks, savings and loans, and credit unions offer these accounts at little or no cost. Brokerage firms offer a similar type of account known as a TOD or transfer-on-death account. At writing, 36 states allow TOD accounts. Check with your broker to see if these accounts are offered in your state. In a Totten trust, you can hold cash, U.S. Treasury securities, and U.S. saving bonds. Securities are permitted in brokerage accounts. Loans are not available on a Totten trust. Such trusts have several advantages in relation to living trusts and to a person's financial situation:

- You can name a co-trustee who will have account access.

- While either you or the co-trustee is living, the beneficiary cannot have access to the funds.

- The account does not pass through probate upon the trustee(s) death.

- You can change your beneficiary at any time.

- The accounts are federally insured by the Federal Deposit Insurance Corporation (FDIC) separately from the trustee's individual accounts. The amount insured is $100,000 for each qualified beneficiary. To gain the "separation," the qualified beneficiary has to be related (for example, spouse, child, sibling, parent, or grandchild of the trustee). If the beneficiary is someone other than one of these individuals (non-qualified), then the account is insured collectively with the owner's other accounts up to $100,000.

There are disadvantages of a Totten trust:

- Only one beneficiary is permitted for a Treasury or brokerage account and no alternates. Banks may allow more than one. This is a less flexible arrangement than the more formal, traditional trust.

- You are not allowed to exclude your spouse and disinherit him or her by naming someone else as beneficiary on your account.

- You can name a minor child as a beneficiary, but it is not a good idea. If you die before he or she reaches the age of majority, a court-ordered individual may be appointed as guardian.

· There may be an estate tax. If so, it must be paid before the funds can be made available to the beneficiary. Before setting up such an account, check on state regulations.

Although many of the more complex trusts described above are not within the scope of this book, we have provided an example of typical, general trust language at the end of this chapter courtesy of the Internal Revenue Service so you can get an idea of how these trust documents are worded.

For a Sample Charitable Trust Form, visit **www.irs.gov/irb/2005-34_IRB/ar06.html.**

Section IV: Sample Inter Vivos Charitable Remainder Unitrust- One Life

On this _____ day of _____, 20___, I, _____ (hereinafter "the Donor"), desiring to establish a charitable remainder unitrust within the meaning of Rev. Proc. 2005-52 and § 664(d)(2) of the Internal Revenue Code (hereinafter "the Code"), hereby enter into this trust agreement with _____ as the initial trustee (hereinafter "the Trustee"). This trust shall be known as the _____ Charitable Remainder Unitrust.

1. Funding of Trust. The Donor hereby transfers and irrevocably assigns, on the above date, to the Trustee the property described in Schedule A, and the Trustee accepts the property and agrees to hold, manage, and distribute the property, and any property subsequently transferred, under the terms set forth in this trust instrument.

2. Payment of Unitrust Amount. In each taxable year of the trust during the unitrust period, the Trustee shall pay to [permissible recipient] (hereinafter "the Recipient") a unitrust amount equal to

Sample Inter Vivos Charitable Remainder Unitrust- One Life

[a number no less than 5 and no more than 50] percent of the net fair market value of the assets of the trust valued as of the first day of each taxable year of the trust (hereinafter "the valuation date"). The first day of the unitrust period shall be the date property is first transferred to the trust and the last day of the unitrust period shall be the date of the Recipient's death. The unitrust amount shall be paid in equal quarterly installments at the end of each calendar quarter from income and, to the extent income is not sufficient, from principal. Any income of the trust for a taxable year in excess of the unitrust amount shall be added to principal. If, for any year, the net fair market value of the trust assets is incorrectly determined, then within a reasonable period after the correct value is finally determined, the Trustee shall pay to the Recipient (in the case of an undervaluation) or receive from the Recipient (in the case of an overvaluation) an amount equal to the difference between the unitrust amount(s) properly payable and the unitrust amount(s) actually paid.

3. Proration of Unitrust Amount. For a short taxable year and for the taxable year during which the unitrust period ends, the Trustee shall prorate on a daily basis the unitrust amount described in paragraph 2, or, if an additional contribution is made to the trust, the unitrust amount described in paragraph 5.

4. Distribution to Charity. At the termination of the unitrust period, the Trustee shall distribute all the then principal and income of the trust (other than any amount due the Recipient under the terms of this trust) to [designated remainderman] (hereinafter "the Charitable Organization"). If the Charitable Organization is not an organization described in §§ 170(c), 2055(a), and 2522(a) of the Code at the time when any principal or income of the trust is to be distributed to it, then the Trustee shall distribute the then principal and income to one or more organizations described in §§ 170(c), 2055(a), and 2522(a) of the Code as the Trustee shall select, and in the proportions as the Trustee shall decide, in the Trustee's sole discretion.

Sample Inter Vivos Charitable Remainder Unitrust- One Life

5. Additional Contributions. If any additional contributions are made to the trust after the initial contribution, the unitrust amount for the year in which any additional contribution is made shall be [same percentage used in paragraph 2] percent of the sum of (a) the net fair market value of the trust assets as of the valuation date (excluding the assets so added and any post-contribution income from, and appreciation on, such assets during that year) and (b) for each additional contribution during the year, the fair market value of the assets so added as of the valuation date (including any post-contribution income from, and appreciation on, such assets through the valuation date) multiplied by a fraction the numerator of which is the number of days in the period that begins with the date of contribution and ends with the earlier of the last day of the taxable year or the last day of the unitrust period and the denominator of which is the number of days in the period that begins with the first day of such taxable year and ends with the earlier of the last day in such taxable year or the last day of the unitrust period. In a taxable year in which an additional contribution is made on or after the valuation date, the assets so added shall be valued as of the date of contribution, without regard to any post-contribution income or appreciation, rather than as of the valuation date.

6. Deferral of the Unitrust Payment Allocable to Testamentary Transfer. All property passing to the trust by reason of the death of the Donor (hereinafter "the testamentary transfer") shall be considered to be a single contribution that is made on the date of the Donor's death. Notwithstanding the provisions of paragraphs 2 and 5 above, the obligation to pay the unitrust amount with respect to the testamentary transfer shall commence with the date of the Donor's death. Nevertheless , payment of the unitrust amount with respect to the testamentary transfer may be deferred from the date of the Donor's death until the end of the taxable year in which the funding of the testamentary transfer is completed. Within a reasonable time

CHAPTER 6: WHAT TYPES OF TRUSTS ARE THERE?

Sample Inter Vivos Charitable Remainder Unitrust- One Life

Within a reasonable time after the end of the taxable year in which the testamentary transfer is completed, the Trustee must pay to the Recipient (in the case of an underpayment) or receive from the Recipient (in the case of an overpayment) the difference between any unitrust amounts allocable to the testamentary transfer that were actually paid, plus interest, and the unitrust amounts allocable to the testamentary transfer that were payable, plus interest. The interest shall be computed for any period at the rate of interest, compounded annually, that the federal income tax regulations under § 664 of the Code prescribe for this computation.

7. Unmarketable Assets. Whenever the value of a trust asset must be determined, the Trustee shall determine the value of any assets that are not cash, cash equivalents, or other assets that can be readily sold or exchanged for cash or cash equivalents (hereinafter "unmarketable assets"), by either (a) obtaining a current "qualified appraisal" from a "qualified appraiser," as defined in § 1.170A-13(c)(3) and § 1.170A-13(c)(5) of the Income Tax Regulations, respectively, or (b) ensuring the valuation of these unmarketable assets is performed exclusively by an "independent trustee," within the meaning of § 1.664-1(a)(7)(iii) of the Income Tax Regulations.

8. Prohibited Transactions. The Trustee shall not engage in any act of self-dealing within the meaning of § 4941(d) of the Code, as modified by § 4947(a)(2)(A) of the Code, and shall not make any taxable expenditures within the meaning of § 4945(d) of the Code, as modified by § 4947(a)(2)(A) of the Code.

9. Taxable Year. The taxable year of the trust shall be the calendar year.

10. Governing Law. The operation of the trust shall be governed by the laws of the State of _____. However, the Trustee is prohibited from exercising any power or discretion granted

Sample Inter Vivos Charitable Remainder Unitrust- One Life

the trust as a charitable remainder unitrust under § 664(d)(2) of the Code and the corresponding regulations.

11. Limited Power of Amendment. This trust is irrevocable. However, the Trustee shall have the power, acting alone, to amend the trust from time to time in any manner required for the sole purpose of ensuring that the trust qualifies and continues to qualify as a charitable remainder unitrust within the meaning of § 664(d)(2) of the Code.

12. Investment of Trust Assets. Nothing in this trust instrument shall be construed to restrict the Trustee from investing the trust assets in a manner that could result in the annual realization of a reasonable amount of income or gain from the sale or disposition of trust assets.

13. Definition of Recipient. References to the Recipient in this trust instrument shall be deemed to include the estate of the Recipient with regard to all provisions in this trust instrument that describe amounts payable to and/or due from the Recipient. The prior sentence shall not apply to the determination of the last day of the unitrust period.

7
Who are the Beneficiaries of a Living Trust?

With a living trust, you are free to choose anyone you want as beneficiaries. The category of beneficiaries will vary with the type of trust.

Individual or Basic Shared Trusts

With these types of trusts, there are three categories of beneficiaries. Primary beneficiaries are the individuals, institutions, or groups whom you have chosen to receive specific property. Contingent (alternate) beneficiaries are those whom you select to receive property left to a primary beneficiary if that primary beneficiary dies before you do. Remainder beneficiaries are those who receive all trust property that is not bequeathed to primary or contingent beneficiaries. Naming beneficiaries for a basic living trust is easy: You simply list them. They can include your spouse, children, friends, young adults, and charities. If you establish a basic living trust, remember that you and your spouse name your beneficiaries separately. That is because each spouse's trust property share is distributed when that spouse dies. When the first spouse dies, that spouse's trust property gets distributed to the beneficiaries he or she named in his or her trust. Upon the second spouse's death, the property in his or her trust is distributed to the second spouse's beneficiaries.

AB Living Trusts

Generally speaking, AB living trusts have two categories of beneficiaries. The life beneficiary is always the surviving spouse. The final beneficiaries are those individuals named by each spouse for his or her property. In effect, final beneficiaries are those named by the deceased spouse to receive the property in Trust A when the surviving spouse dies. More simply put, each spouse names his or her trust beneficiaries. Then, when the surviving spouse dies, the beneficiaries of the previously deceased spouse will receive their designated assets, and the beneficiaries of the surviving spouse (now also deceased) will receive their designated assets. The naming of specific beneficiaries is not as much of a concern with AB Trusts. That is because the bulk of the property is left in Trust A and that means to your surviving spouse, who can use it during his or her lifetime. Each spouse does select final beneficiaries, but they inherit the property only upon the death of the second spouse. If you use an AB Disclaimer Trust, however, the beneficiaries selected by the deceased spouse cannot inherit that spouse's trust property if the surviving spouse does not disclaim trust property and create Trust A. Most often, when spouses are in their first marriage, they both select the same final beneficiaries. Of course, it is different when spouses have children from previous marriages. Then they often name different beneficiaries. A general rule on beneficiaries is: If you or your spouse is thinking of naming different beneficiaries, make sure they will all get along. This can head off a lot of conflict and tension among those beneficiaries. You also have the option of naming alternate beneficiaries in the event a final beneficiary dies before you do.

Simultaneous Death Clauses

The chances of the simultaneous death of spouses are of a low statistical probability. However, if this is a concern, an appropriate clause can be inserted in the living trust document. Essentially, this clause states that, if both spouses die at the same time, then property of each spouse is distributed as if he or she had survived the other. Simultaneous death clauses in the United States have their origins in the Uniform Simultaneous Death Act. You can find information on the history of the statute and its applications at this Web site: **http://en.wikipedia.org/ wiki/Uniform_Simultaneous_Death_Act**.

Shared Gifts

If you wish, you can name multiple beneficiaries for any item of property in your trust. This is a "shared gift." Often, the beneficiaries of shared gifts are children. You can name more than one beneficiary to inherit any item of trust property, whether it is real estate, land, stocks, or bonds. One caution: Be sure to list the specific names of the all children in the trust document. Do not be vague and use terms like "my children." This can result in legal confusion and results you might not like if a primary beneficiary dies before you do. Also, another caution: Make sure the children will get along if you bequeath property that cannot be physically divided (a home, for example). Obviously, if they do not get along, legal fights could erupt over the management or sale of such properties, and family harmony would suffer. In any event, it is best to be crystal clear about your intentions in the trust document. One way to do this is to establish percentage of ownership. Let us assume you have a stock portfolio and want your two children to share equally. In that case, you can specify the following:

The grantor's two children, Daniel Smith and Jan Smith, shall each be given equal shares in the Putnam Aggressive Growth fund.

Or, perhaps, you also have a house and want to divide it differently among your spouse and children. In this instance, you can specify a division similar to the following: The grantor's spouse and children shall be given the grantor's interest in the grantor's house and lot known as 1234 Elm Street, Chicago, Illinois in the following shares:

60 percent to the grantor's spouse, Emily

20 percent to the grantor's son, Dan

20 percent to the grantor's daughter, Jan

Percentage of ownership can be applied to many items in your living trust, such as jewelry. Just be sure to stick to percentages, and do not define shared gifts in dollar amounts. It is a fact that you most likely will not know how much your property is worth at the time of your death. It could be worth more, or it could be worth less. If it is less, then the property might not be valuable enough to pay those dollar amounts you specified. On one hand, if the value is more, there may be money left over and conflict can erupt over that. As a general rule, if you are going to specify dollar amounts, limit it to liquid assets like bank accounts or money market funds.

One possible difficulty with shared ownership is conflict among the beneficiaries. You may be able to head this off by discussing it with the beneficiaries you have selected to receive the property. If you find there is harmony among them, then you have no problem. You can simply bequeath the shared gift without any conditions or directions. On the other hand, if you find there is "dissension in the ranks," then you may want to put in specific provisions regarding the property in question. For example, you may want to state: "My home at 123 Elm Street, Omaha, Nebraska, may not be sold unless all four of my children agree upon the sale." This may not head off all potential conflict, but at least you are clear in your wishes. A final note on this subject: If you are reasonably sure that conflict will arise among the beneficiaries, then do not make a shared gift in the first place.

Additional Information on Beneficiaries

Depending upon the kind of living trust you establish, you will have to make certain choices when it comes to naming your beneficiaries.

Remember, with a basic living trust, you can name only one individual (or institution) as your primary beneficiary. In many cases, one spouse wants to name his or her spouse as the primary beneficiary. If this is your choice, you then name your spouse by listing him or her as the sole primary beneficiary. Or you can do the same thing by leaving everything in your residuary clause to the residuary beneficiary. Also remember that, if you establish an AB Trust, most or all of each spouse's property must be left to Trust A.

But what happens when you leave property to a beneficiary who is married? In that case, the gift is the named person's property. It is not shared marital property. If you stipulate in the trust that "Emmanuel Jones shall be given my rare coin collection," then the collection belongs to him and him alone. On the other hand, if you wish to leave the gift to a married couple, then list both of their names, such as "Emmanuel and Ruth Jones shall be given my rare coin collection."

Now what happens if you or your spouse has children from a previous marriage? There are a number of ways to leave gifts to them. One choice is to simply leave them gifts outright. This can be done using either a basic living trust or a standard AB Trust. You can also create a life estate using a standard AB Trust. In this case, you list children from a prior marriage as final beneficiaries. Generally speaking, each child gets a set percentage of the remaining trust property after your spouse dies. If you see the potential for conflict, hire a lawyer to work out the details.

In the case of a minor (under 18) or young adult beneficiaries, you will need to choose an adult to manage the trust property. Remember, management only takes effect if the beneficiary is too young to sensibly manage property when he or she inherits it.

What if you want to leave property to the successor trustee? It is very common and completely legal. Remember, often the successor trustee is a child or other relative, so it can make sense to leave the property to him or her.

If you have pets, you can also provide for them in your living trust. For example, assume you have a beloved Springer spaniel named Max, and you want to make sure he is well cared for in the event of your death. You can name him in the trust and provide expense money for his care. Naturally, you will want to give him to someone who cares about pets as much as you do, so choose a person who will willingly take Max and be sure to inform them of your decision. Needless to say, you do not want to surprise a person with the gift of a dog when they could care less about pets. It would not be fair to Max or the recipient.

8
How Do I Leave Property to Minor Children or Young Adults?

When leaving property to minor children or young adults, you need to have someone manage that property for them. This is especially important if they are liable to inherit that property before they are able to manage it in a responsible manner. A minor child is defined as any beneficiary under the age of 18. By law, they cannot directly manage large amounts of money. These amounts are defined by individual states and may range from amount exceeding $2,500 to $5,000. It is important to name an adult to manage the trust property because if you do not, the court will appoint a guardian to perform that task. It is for you to nominate a guardian, and that nomination must be done through your will; it cannot be done through your living trust.

You can also nominate a custodian for any beneficiary over 18 years of age if you believe he or she is not mature enough to handle gifts from your living trust. This is an individual decision, of course. Young adults may handle money well, or they may lack maturity and run through their inheritance in short order.

There are several options you can choose from to leave property to a minor or young adult.

Child's Trust

You have the option of creating one or more child's trusts in your living trust. You do this by creating a separate "sub trust" for each child or young adult. When such trusts are created, the successor trustee manages the property in them. He or she uses the trust to take care of the beneficiary's health, education, and other needs. In the case of a shared living trust or an AB living trust, the surviving spouse manages the property left to minors by the deceased spouse. Only after both spouses have died does the successor trustee take over. You can also name a specific age at which the remaining trust property is turned over to the beneficiary.

THE UNIFORM GIFTS TO MINORS ACT

The Uniform Gifts to Minors Act, known as UGMA, is an act in some states of the United States that allows assets such as securities, where the donor has given up all possession and control, to be held in the custodian's name for the benefit of the minor without an attorney needing to set up a special trust fund. This allows minors in the United States to have property set aside for their benefit and may achieve income tax benefit for the child's parents. After the child reaches the age of majority (18 or 21 depending on the state), the assets become the property of the child and the child can use them for whatever purpose he or she chooses.

In states that have adopted the Uniform Transfers To Minors Act (UTMA), the assets may be treated similarly: the assets are held in the custodian's name until the child reaches age of majority. States that adopted UTMA also repealed UGMA; UTMA specifically provides that contracts in UTMA states which reference UGMA are governed by UTMA. Thus, UGMA is still referred to in contracts designed for use in multiple states, though it may actually mean UTMA in a particular state.

THE UNIFORM GIFTS TO MINORS ACT

The Internal Revenue Service of the United States allows persons to give up to the annual gift tax exclusion to another person without any gift tax consequences. If this recipient person is a minor, the UGMA or UTMA allows the assets to be held in the custodian's name for the benefit of the minor without an attorney setting up a special trust fund. Under the UGMA or UTMA, the ownership of the funds works like it does with any other trust except that the donor must appoint a custodian (the trustee) to look after the account.

A UGMA or UTMA account allows the assets to be taxed at the minor's income tax bracket. With the increase in the age from 14 to 18 where the kiddie tax is imposed, the tax advantage of a UGMA or UTMA is decreased. As of 2007 only about $1,700 of the child's unearned income can avoid being taxed at the child's parent's tax rate.

Leave the Property Directly to a Responsible Adult

With this option you can leave the property to a child's parents or to an individual expected to have custody of that child in the event neither parent is available. This is not a legal arrangement, so you need to have complete trust in the adult and be sure they will use the property wisely for the benefit of the child.

Uniform Transfers to Minors Act (UTMA)

A panel of national experts wrote this model law, and it has been adopted by many states. The exceptions are South Carolina and Vermont. If you live in a state with a UTMA, you may use your living trust to name a custodian, who will manage the property you leave to a child until that child reaches the specified age as determined by state law. The UTMA is an extension of the Uniform Gifts to Minors Act (UGMA).

The UTMA and custodianships are simpler, cheaper, and easier than a child's trust. States may have custodial powers written into their laws so institutions such as banks and insurance companies are familiar with the rules. Trusts can vary widely in their terms, and a financial institution's demand to analyze the terms of the trust. Custodianships also may be more flexible. Unlike a child's trust, you can name anyone to be a custodian. You may be able to get better income tax rates with a custodianship as well. UTMA property managed by a custodian is taxed as income paid directly to the child, and this may be a lower rate than that paid by a trust. With a child's trust, you pay 15 percent tax on retained income up to $1,950 annually with the top rate reaching 35 percent on income over $9,500. Custodianships are explored in more depth later in this chapter.

The child's trust allows the assets to be managed for a longer time and prevents any foolish spending by a beneficiary who is not mature enough to handle money. Either option works well, so choose the one that works best for your situation.

Creating a Child's Trust

First, stipulate gifts in your living trust that are to be left to any children or young adults (life insurance proceeds, for example). Then, complete the child's trust clause. In this clause you list each child's name and the age at which the beneficiary is to receive their trust property outright. If, upon your death, the beneficiary is younger than the specified age, a trust will be created for that beneficiary. If he or she is older, then they get the trust property outright, and no trust is created. Here is a brief example:

> Alice creates a living trust, and one of the beneficiaries is her son Samuel. Within the trust, Alice establishes a child's trust clause. This clause stipulates that Sam will receive his trust property when he reaches age 30. Alice dies when Sam is 23. His property is maintained in the trust until he reaches age 30.

When a child's trust goes into effect, the successor trustee (or surviving spouse if the trust was made together) will need to get a trust ID number for each child's trust. The successor trustee must manage each trust on an individual basis. He or she will be required to file separate tax returns and maintain separate accountings and records for each of the trusts.

You can set up child's trusts with an AB Trust by making up to three specific gifts and naming alternate beneficiaries for each gift. Then, if one or more of these beneficiaries is a minor or young adult, you can create a child's trust for each of them.

Choosing a Trustee of a Child's Trust

Your successor trustee is the trustee for each child's trust unless it is a shared or AB Trust with your spouse. In the latter case, the spouse is the trustee. After both spouses are deceased, the successor trustee assumes operational control of the child's trust. If you want to name someone other than your successor trustee to be custodian, choose the UTMA option (unless you live in

South Carolina or Vermont where you do not have that option). The powers and responsibilities of the trustee should be spelled out in the trust document. Such duties include:

- Management of the child's trust property until the beneficiary reaches the age specified in the trust document.

- Use of the child's trust income or property to pay for the beneficiary's expenses (support, health care, education, and others).

- Maintenance of separate records of all trust transactions.

- Filing of income tax returns for the trust.

- Periodic reports to the beneficiary (depending on the state you are in).

As with other trusts, the trustee of a child's trust is entitled to receive reasonable compensation for his or her work managing the trust. When the beneficiary reaches the designated age, the trustee must give the remaining trust assets to that beneficiary.

Naming Minor Children As Life Insurance Proceeds Beneficiaries

You can name each child as a beneficiary of the proceeds by naming your living trust as the life insurance beneficiary. Specify the amount or percentage each child will receive. Within your living trust, create a separate child's trust for each child. Your living trust does not become the owner of your life insurance policy; you still are the owner. However, if you die while your child or children are below the specified age, then the money will be managed for your offspring by the successor trustee until the children are old enough to receive the money outright. To pass the proceeds of a life insurance through your living trust, you need to name the trustee (as trustee of the child's trust within the living trust) as the beneficiary of your policy. Your insurance agency has forms to allow you to change the policy beneficiary. In your list of property items within your living trust, list the proceeds of the policy, but not the policy itself.

Custodianships

You can create a custodianship for a gift under the Uniform Transfers to Minors Act if you find a UTMA preferable to the creation of a child's trust. In terms of a living trust, you can create as many custodianships as you want for minor or young adult beneficiaries. To do this, identify the property, the beneficiary it is bequeathed to, and name a custodian who will be responsible for supervising the particular property. You also have the option of naming an alternate custodian in case your first choice is not available. Then list the age at which the minor will receive the property outright. In your state you may have no choice in determining that age, and you will have to list the one required by your state. Your named custodian will manage the trust property for the beneficiary until he or she reaches the age specified by the state. At that point, the custodianship ends.

State laws regarding the age at which custodianships end can change and could affect the custodianships you have set up. So, for example, if your state raises the age, the new age determines when the custodianship of the beneficiary terminates. Or if you live in a state with a flexible age range, then you can amend your living trust to reflect the desired age within that range. However, if you do not amend it, the custodianship ends when the beneficiary attains the youngest age allowed under state law.

If you move from one UTMA state to another, little happens to the custodianships you have set up. You can keep your UTMA clause as it is, unless you have moved to a state that stipulates a lower age for turning property over to a minor than the one allowed in your previous state. If the age is different you will have to amend the trust to establish a new age. If you move into one of the exception states, you may have to revise your living trust. In this case, you create children's trusts for any gifts previously made using a custodian. You can still use the UTMA law if the beneficiary or the custodian remains in the UTMA state.

The duties of a custodian are similar to those of a trustee of a child's trust. He or she is required to manage the beneficiary's property in a wise and honest manner. In addition, your state will set out custodial duties and authority in the UTMA document. In general, the duties will look like this:

- Management of the child's property until the beneficiary reaches the age specified in the state's UTMA document.

- Use of the child's income or property to pay for the beneficiary's expenses (support, health care, education, and other expenses).

- Keep the property separate from the custodian's property.

- Maintenance of separate records of all UTMA transactions. (Unlike a child's trust, the custodian does not have to file a separate income tax return. Instead, income from the property is reported on the beneficiary's return.)

As with a child's trust, the custodian has the authority to hire an accountant, tax lawyer, or other expert to aid in management of the UTMA. Payment for such services comes from the managed property. The custodian is also entitled to reasonable compensation and reimbursement for his or services if state law allows it.

It is best to name a custodian who has physical custody of the minor child. This may be one of the child's parents. If the beneficiary is your child, name your spouse as the custodian unless you feel that person will not handle the property in a responsible manner. Only one person can be named as a custodian for one beneficiary. However, you have the option of naming an alternate custodian if the first named custodian cannot assume the responsibility. You can also name different custodians for different beneficiaries.

Children's trusts and custodianships have been the main subject of this chapter. But you can plan strategically to save taxes by using two federal government educational investment plans — the 529 plan and the Coverdell account. By establishing one of these plans, you prevent the drain of money from your estate.

The 529 Plan

A 529 plan is an investment account. It is called a "529" because it was created by that section of the Internal Revenue Code. It is established for the higher education of a named beneficiary, who must be a family member. A family member can be anyone from your own children to cousins. In a 529 plan, income accumulates free of taxes. Even better, no income tax is assessed on money spent to pay for the beneficiary's books, equipment, fees, supplies, and tuition necessary to attend college, graduate school, or approved vocational institutions. With a 529 plan, you can also authorize expenses for disadvantaged students requiring special services.

For any one beneficiary, you can give up to $11,000 per year free from gift tax to a 529 plan, and contributions can be made only in cash. A couple can double the amount to $22,000 per year. If you contribute any amount over these limits within a year, it is subject to federal gift tax.

Federal law requires investments only in a state-authorized plan, so each state has its own plan. These plans are managed by an investment company or companies named by the state. State 529 plan regulations vary. Sometimes a plan will allow you to invest only if you live in the state. Others allow you to deduct 529 contributions from state income tax. However, the plan may allow anyone to invest in it, and you have the option of creating more than one.

There are potential disadvantages to 529 plans. You are investing in securities (stocks and bonds), and the stock market can fluctuate. Also, the management of a 529 plan is important. Managers can be risk-takers, which can result in big rewards or devastating losses. Do your research on a 529 plan and its management before you create one. The U.S. Securities and Exchange Commission recommends the following questions on its Web site (**www.sec.gov/investor/pubs/intro529.htm**):

- Is the plan available directly from the state or plan sponsor?

- What fees are charged by the plan? How much of my investment goes to compensating my broker? Under what circumstances does the plan waive or reduce certain fees?

- What are the plan's withdrawal restrictions?

- What types of college expenses are covered by the plan? Which colleges and universities participate in the plan?

- What types of investment options are offered by the plan? How long are contributions held before being invested?

- Does the plan offer special benefits for state residents? Would I be better off investing in my state's plan or another plan? Does my state's plan offer tax advantages or other benefits for investment in the plan it sponsors? If my state's plan charges higher fees than another state's plan, do the tax advantages or other benefits offered by my state outweigh the benefit of investing in another state's less expensive plan?

- What limitations apply to the plan?

- When can an account holder change investment options, switch beneficiaries, or transfer ownership of the account to another account holder?

- Who is the program manager? When does the program manager's current management contract expire?

- How has the plan performed in the past?

Another disadvantage is if the beneficiary does not attend a college or other approved institution — and the money is taken out for non-educational purposes — taxes and penalties apply.

The Coverdell Account

Another option for saving taxes is a Coverdell account (also called an ESA or Educational Savings Account). The program is named after Senator Paul Coverdell of Georgia. You can contribute up to $2,000 per year (although the contribution amounts phase out for people with six-figure incomes) into a Coverdell account. This is the total amount that can be contributed in any one year for a beneficiary. You cannot have different family members contribute $2,000 to that account (although they can combine their contributions to reach the $2,000 limit). These contributions are not tax-deductible when they are made. The advantage of a Coverdell is after the money is in the account, it is not taxed as it grows. In addition, no tax is due when you make qualified withdrawals to pay for a child's educational expenses. The disadvantage of a Coverdell is the $2,000 limit. That is why more parents use 529 plans. The account must be fully withdrawn by the time the beneficiary reaches age 30, or it will be subject to tax and penalties.

The **www.wikipedia.com** Web site provides the following comparison of 529 plans with Coverdell accounts:

IMPORTANT DIFFERENCES WITH 529 PLAN

1. Coverdell ESAs have lower contribution limits; currently $2,000 can be contributed per year per child, while 529 plans generally have no restrictions on contributions. (Gift tax rules apply.)

2. Coverdell ESAs can allow almost any investment inside including stocks, bonds, and mutual funds, while 529 plans only allow a choice among a number of state-run allocation programs. The rules for investments allowed in ESAs are the same as those for IRAs.

3. Balances in a Coverdell ESA must be disbursed on qualified education expenses by the time the beneficiary is 30 years old or gifted to another family member below the age of 30 to avoid taxes and penalties; there is no age limit for 529 plans.

4. Coverdell ESAs allow withdrawing the money tax free for qualified elementary and secondary school expenses; 529 plans do not.

5. The income level of a donor may affect contributions into a Coverdell ESA, but would not affect contributions to a Section 529 plan.

IMPORTANT SIMILARITIES WITH 529 PLANS

1. Money in both a Coverdell ESA and a 529 plan is not considered the child's (beneficiary's) money when applying for federal financial aid as long as the owner of the account is someone other than the beneficiary, such as a parent. This works to increase the child's potential financial aid because parents are expected to contribute only around 6 percent of their assets to finance college education, as opposed to the child's 35 percent.

2. The custodian of both an ESA and a 529 plan can designate a new beneficiary without incurring taxes or penalties as long as the new beneficiary is an eligible family member of the previous beneficiary.

9
What Are the Responsibilities of the Successor Trustee?

The successor trustee is the administrator of your trust; he or she manages the assets you have placed in your living trust. The powers and responsibilities of the trustee are described in the living trust. It is crucial they be spelled out in detail. Poorly written or vague powers can lead to abuse or mismanagement of the trust assets. A successor trustee is responsible for conferring property to your beneficiaries. He or she is also responsible for handling any other matters specified in the trust. In addition, the successor trustee can appoint a co-trustee to help with trust details. Several states also impose specific duties on the successor trustee. After he or she takes over administration of a living trust, the co-trustee should be aware of state law regarding those duties.

A successor trustee's duties depend on the type of living trust that has been established. Below is an overview of those duties for different types of trusts:

Duties of a Successor Trustee for an Individual Trust

Upon the death of the grantor (the initial trustee), the successor trustee takes over the trust. He or she then has the responsibility of distributing the property to the beneficiaries' named in the individual trust; however, the trustee does not have the responsibility to sell or manage the property in the trust. The successor trustee also must manage the trust property left in a child's trust (if any) and file state and federal tax returns as necessary. If there is a will, this is also the responsibility of the executor of the estate.

Duties of a Successor Trustee for a Basic Shared Living Trust

This trust splits automatically into two separate trusts upon the death of a spouse. So Trust 1 holds the deceased spouse's share of trust property (excluding any trust property this person has left to the surviving spouse). The terms of Trust 1 cannot be changed or revoked. Trust 2 holds the surviving spouse's trust property. This includes any of the deceased spouse's trust property left to the survivor. Since Trust 2 belongs to the surviving spouse, he or she can amend the terms of this trust or even revoke it. In this situation, the surviving spouse is the sole trustee of Trust 1, Trust 2, and any child's trusts set up for the deceased's beneficiaries.

The trustee is responsible for distributing the property of your deceased spouse to the named beneficiaries. If there is a child's trust, the trustee must manage that as well. The trustee must also file state and federal estate tax returns, (if necessary). If there is a will, this is also the executor's responsibility. The trustee also has the ability to amend Trust 2 to reflect any changed circumstances.

Duties of a Successor Trustee for AB Trusts

Both spouses are the original trustees of either the AB or AB disclaimer trusts. The surviving spouse becomes sole trustee when his or her spouse dies. In the case of a standard AB Trust, the living trust splits into two trusts. These trusts are the irrevocable Trust A of the deceased spouse and the revocable Trust B of the surviving spouse. With an AB Disclaimer Trust, on the other hand, Trust A is created only if the survivor disclaims trust property. If Trust A is created, there is no need for a new trust document, except for the preparation of new schedules listing the properties in Trust A and B. If you are the survivor (and trustee), you will need to prepare two new schedules. One will list all property held in Trust A. The other will list all property contained in Trust B (property owned by you). All properties should be listed and described in detail so the Internal Revenue Service is clear on which property belongs in which trust.

As trustee, it is your responsibility to distribute any property of your deceased spouse to specific beneficiaries. You must then maintain the remainder of the property in the ongoing Trust A. You are required to file a Trust A tax return every year and give copies to the beneficiaries (if required by the trust). In addition, you must manage the property in a child's trust (if any) and file any necessary state and federal tax returns. If there is a will, this is also the responsibility of the executor. If necessary, you can amend Trust B to reflect changing circumstances.

With AB Trusts, division of property between Trust A and Trust B after one spouse has died can be a complicated affair and may require the aid of an expert to get the best tax benefits. You can allocate it any way you want as long as each trust gets 50 percent of the total worth. For example, an asset worth $500,000 can be placed in Trust A as long as other co-owned property worth $500,000 is placed in Trust B. Confusion and complications can arise when each spouse names different beneficiaries for their portions of shared-ownership property.

Transference of Property Procedures

Procedures for transferring property depend on the nature of the beneficiaries. With a basic living trust, the property left by a deceased spouse stays in the trust, and no action is required. With an AB trust, the Trust A property must be clearly identified as belonging to that trust. The property left to Trust B by the deceased spouse stays in the ongoing living trust, and no action is required. In terms of beneficiaries, trust property left to them must be actually transferred to their possession. With a child's trust, any property left to the young beneficiary remains in that trust until the child attains the age to receive the trust property outright, and under the UTMA, the property left to the custodian must be given to the custodian named in the trust document.

To get the trust property, it is necessary for the trustee to obtain a copy of the grantor's death certificate and a copy of the trust document. If both grantors are deceased, then copies of both death certificates will be required. An Affidavit of Assumption of Duties by the Successor Trustee may also be required. Other paperwork may be involved as well. Since paperwork from banks and stock brokerages can be complicated and vary from state to state, the trustee has the authority to get help from experts. Such experts may include lawyers, accountants, and others. The trustee can pay for expert advice from the trust's assets.

Trust properties may not have title documents, such as furniture, fixtures, and others. In this case, transference is a simple matter. The trustee distributes them to the beneficiaries named in the trust document as promptly as possible. The trustee may want signed receipts for these properties as a matter of record. This may not be necessary when family members have trust in one another.

Bank Accounts/Savings and Loan Accounts

In terms of bank or savings and loan accounts, it can be a simple procedure to transfer the funds to the beneficiary, since these institutions are familiar with living trusts. To initiate the transfer, the trustee needs to show the bank or savings and loan certain documents of proof. These include a certified copy of the trust grantor's death certificate, a copy of the living trust document (if the bank or savings and loan do not already have one), and proof of his or her identify (which may include an Affidavit of Assumption of Duties by Successor Trustee).

Stocks, Bonds, and Government Securities

Transfer of stocks or bonds to a beneficiary depends on how

they are held. If the financial instruments are in a brokerage account, the successor trustee should contact the firm and request instructions. The brokerage may already have a copy of the living trust document or a form with similar information, since they were necessary to transfer the account to the living trust in the first place. In the rare event these forms are not in the possession of the brokerage, the trustee should send the firm a copy of the trust document or an Abstract of Trust (called a Certification of Trust depending on the state you live in).

An Abstract of Trust is a summary of the living trust document. Its purpose is to prove to the brokerage or other financial institution that a valid living trust was established. The abstract does not reveal any private information or the identity of the beneficiaries. It may be two or three pages long and contains the notarized signature. Along with the copy of the living trust document or Abstract of Trust, the successor trustee should send a letter that instructs the firm to transfer the brokerage account to the beneficiary.

In the case of stock certificates, the successor trustee should contact the transfer agent for instructions. This is easy, since the name and address of the agent is normally printed on the stock or bond certificate. However, agents do change, so the trustee should contact the firm to verify the name and address of the current transfer agent. To effectively transfer the securities to the beneficiary, the successor trustee may have to provide the following documents:

- A certified copy of the grantor's death certificate

- A "stock or bond power" document. This is evidence of a shareholder's intention to transfer ownership of the security. The trustee has to fill it out and sign it with the signature guaranteed by a bank or brokerage officer.

· An Affidavit of Domicile. This specifies the trust grantor's state of residence. It must be signed by the trustee.

· A letter of instructions. This requests that the certificates be reissued in the beneficiary's name.

For government securities, the trustee will need to contact the appropriate government agency.

If mutual funds or money market accounts are involved, the trustee will need to contact the company to determine what is required to re-register ownership of the account in the beneficiary's name. The trustee may have to provide proof of their identity, a copy of the grantor's death certificate, a letter of instructions, and a copy of the trust document.

If a living trust contains small business interests, the nature of the transfer will depend on the organization of these businesses (in alphabetical order):

· **Closely Held Corporations and Limited Liability Companies (LLCs).** In this instance, the stock certificates or ownership interest owned by the trust must be re-issued in the beneficiary's name. The trustee will have to contact corporation or LLC officers. Under a corporation's bylaws or a shareholder agreement, the other shareholders or owners may have the right to buy back the shares or interest.

- **Partnerships**. The trustee will have to contact the partners of the deceased grantor. They may have the right to buy out the grantor's share. Of course, the beneficiary may want to enter into the partnership. If so, then the partnership agreement must be altered to add the beneficiary.

- **Sole Proprietorships**. As with any other trust property, the trustee must transfer business assets to the beneficiary. If the name of the business itself is owned by the living trust, then the trustee should not have to do anything to transfer it to the beneficiary.

- **Solely Owned Corporations**. In this case, corporation officers need to show that ownership has been transferred to the beneficiary by preparing the appropriate corporate documents. The forms of these documents will vary according to the company bylaws and incorporation papers. Once the paperwork is completed, the trustee must then have the stock certificates re-issued in the beneficiary's name.

Other property to be transferred may include copyrights and patents. Since the U.S. Copyright Office provides no forms for transfer, the trustee will need to sign and file a document transferring all the copyright rights in the trust to the beneficiary. If the trustee has executed a transfer and wishes to record the document, see Circular 12, Recordations of Transfers and Other Documents (**http://www.copyright. gov/circs/circ12.pdf**) for an example. With patents, the transfer process is somewhat different. The trustee prepares an "assignment" document and records it with the U.S. Patent and Trademark Office (**http://www.uspto.gov**). Recording the transfer requires a small fee.

What should be done if there are other items in the trust with title documents that show ownership in the name of the trust? In this instance, the trustee has to prepare and sign a new title document transferring ownership to the beneficiary. If the property is in the possession of someone else, normally he or she will need to provide a copy of the trust document and of the trust grantor's death certificate.

Tax Returns

Current circumstances will dictate the tax return forms the successor trustee must file. These may include:

- Federal estate tax return for the deceased grantor (if the value of the estate is beyond the estate tax threshold for the year of death)

- A state estate tax return (if required by state law)

- Final federal income tax return/state income tax return (if applicable) for the deceased grantor

- Final federal income tax return/state income tax return (if applicable) for Trust A after both spouses die

Filing these returns is the legal responsibility of both the successor trustee and the executor named in the deceased grantor's will (possibly the same person). State and federal income tax returns are due April 15 of the year following the grantor's death. The federal estate tax return is due nine months after the grantor's death. Since tax law can be quite complicated, the successor trustee may pay for professional help to deal with these matters. He or she is entitled to pay these fees out of trust assets.

Administration of a Child's Trust

If the beneficiary is not old enough to receive a trust outright, the successor trustee must manage the trust assets until the specified age is reached. A child's trust comes into being only if, at the grantor's death, the beneficiary has not yet reached the age specified by the grantor. Here is an example of how this works:

> Sally sets up a living trust. She names her two young children — Bob and Jane — as beneficiaries. She makes this specification: If either child is younger than 25 when she dies, the property inherited should be kept in separate children's trusts. Upon Sally's death, Bob is 27 and Jane is 22. Since Bob is two years over the specified 25 age, he gets his property outright. However, Jane is three years under the specified age. Therefore, the successor trustee is responsible for managing her property and turning it over to her when she reaches the age of 25.

Administration of a Custodianship

Custodianship duties for a successor trustee are similar to those for a child's trust. The UTMA, as adopted by a specific state's legislature, spells out the custodian's duties.

10
How Do I Transfer Property to My Living Trust?

Your living trust does not take effect until your property is listed in the trust property schedule. Simply writing the living trust document is not enough. All property, such as bank accounts, stocks, and real estate, must be transferred into the trust. This is not difficult for you to accomplish on your own without the help of a lawyer. You will need to complete the necessary paperwork for each item of property. Property can be categorized into two areas — property without document of title and property with a document of title.

Property without document of title includes items such as appliances, books, clothing, and furniture. Since these items do not have titles, you simply list them in the property schedule in nearly all states. This is done with an "Assignment of Property Form." This form can be written up for one person or for a couple with shared property or an AB Trust. Your state may allow a written assignment of property without documents and titles as proof of ownership. However, if you have these items, it may be a good idea to include them since it establishes certainty of ownership. Also, be sure to check your state laws regarding the assignment of property without document of title.

Property with document of title has quite different requirements. In this case, you will need to write new documents to establish trust ownership of the property.

Abstract of Trust

An abstract of trust is a summary of the living trust document. It leaves out details of the trust and the identity of the beneficiaries. Its purpose is to prove to banks and other institutions that you have established a valid living trust, without revealing specifics that you want to keep private. Depending on the state you live in, this document could have a different name: Certification of Trust. Check with your state to see if there is a form you have to complete. There may not be such a requirement, but it does not hurt to make sure so you do not run into problems later.

11
What Happens After the Grantor Dies?

When the grantor of a living trust dies, the property in the trust is transferred to the beneficiaries or placed in an individual trust, AB (bypass) trust, disclaimer trust, or other type of trust. Responsibility for the transfer depends on the type of trust. If you created an individual living trust, the transfer responsibility falls to your successor trustee and then alternate successor trustees (if necessary). If it is a basic shared living trust or an AB trust, then the responsibility belongs to your surviving spouse followed by successor trustee(s) and alternate successor trustee(s).

Multiple Successor Trustees

When there is more than one successor trustee, the responsibilities are shared. The terms of the trust determine if they must formally agree on any actions taken regarding the property in the living trust.

Resignation of a Trustee

A trustee can resign at any time. He or she must provide a

signed and notarized statement of resignation and then deliver that statement to the individual who is next in line to serve as trustee. It could read similar to the example below:

RESIGNATION NOTICE

I am John T. Jones, and I am a current trustee of the Adam Adams Living Trust dated September 16th, 20__. I wish to inform you that I am resigning as trustee effective immediately.

Date: January 21, 20__

After this person resigns, someone else must be appointed to take over his or her responsibilities. Whoever is chosen, their appointment has to be in writing, and it must be signed and notarized.

Removing a Trustee

Although it rarely happens, a trustee can be removed. If a beneficiary becomes upset with the manner in which a trustee is handling the trust property, the beneficiary has two choices. He or she can try to work out the dispute with the trustee, or he or she can file a lawsuit to attempt to force the trustee's removal. Your trust should have a provision that you (as creator of the trust) retain the right to remove a trustee at any time with or without cause. Since it is your trust, you should stipulate that you have the right to remove the current trustee and replace him or her with another person or institution.

A more thorny issue is whether the trust beneficiaries should have the right to remove a trustee after your death. Beneficiaries have conflicting interests or conflicts with each other. This is not a problem easily solved, but if a trustee is not carrying out his or her duties as stipulated in the trust, then that person should be removed. However, if the beneficiaries are bent on taking actions that conflict with your intentions for the trust, then they should not have the opportunity to remove the trustee. One solution is to limit the choice of a successor trustee. For example, you can stipulate if the trustee is removed that the successor trustee must be a specific individual or institution. This requirement may help ensure your intentions for the trust are carried out properly.

Trustee Duties and Responsibilities

There are two basic tasks trustees must complete when they assume responsibility for your living trust. First, they need to write and record an "Affidavit of Assumption of Duties of Successor Trustee," though the specific document title vary by state. This may done at the county land records office. There is no standard form for this affidavit, but it should include the following information:

1. The name of the trust

2. The date the trust document was signed

3. The name of the person who is becoming the successor trustee

A certified copy of the grantor's death certificate should also be attached. These are available from the county or state vital records department.

The second task is to assume the specific responsibilities

of the trust itself. Since trusts vary, the successor trustee's responsibilities vary as well.

Responsibilities and Duties for Individual Trusts

The successor trustee named for the trust takes over when the grantor (also the trustee) dies. It is the responsibility of the successor trustee to distribute the trust property to the named beneficiaries. It is not the duty of the successor trustee to manage or sell the property. The successor trustee must file any required federal and state estate tax returns. The trust exists only as long as it takes to allocate the trust property to the beneficiaries. On the grantor's death, this may take a few weeks. After distribution of all property is accomplished, the trust comes to an end. With a child's trust, the successor's duties may continue for years or until the beneficiary reaches the age specified in the document. As noted in earlier chapters, the Uniform Transfer to Minors Act (UTMA) has a different structure. A custodian manages any property inherited by a young beneficiary. He or she receives that property and has responsibility for it. The successor trustee can also be named custodian of the UTMA property.

Responsibilities and Duties for Basic Shared Living Trusts

On the death of one spouse, there is an automatic split of a basic shared living trust into two separate trusts. Trust 1 holds the deceased spouse's share of trust property with the exclusion of any trust property he or she left to the surviving spouse. Trust 1 terms cannot be changed or revoked. Trust 2 holds the surviving spouse's trust property. This includes any of the deceased spouse's shares of that property. Unlike

Trust 1, Trust 2 can be amended or revoked by the surviving spouse. The surviving spouse is the sole trustee of both trusts and of any children's trusts set up by the deceased spouse's young beneficiaries. The surviving spouse is responsible for distributing the property from Trust 1 to the beneficiaries named in that trust. Trust 1 property may be left to the surviving spouse so there is little in the way of duties and responsibilities, because the trust property inherited is already in the revocable Trust 2. The trust property does not go to the surviving spouse. It stays in the trust. Because Trust 2 is revocable, the surviving spouse can change it as he or she wishes. The successor trustee is responsible for filing any required federal and state estate tax returns.

Responsibilities and Duties for AB (Bypass) Trusts

In a standard AB trust, the trust is divided into two: the irrevocable Trust A of the deceased spouse and Trust B, the revocable trust of the surviving spouse. An important key in the administration of an AB trust after the death of the first spouse is to document everything thoroughly so the trust will survive the scrutiny of the Internal Revenue Service. The IRS should be able to determine with relative ease which property belongs to Trust A and which belongs to Trust B. The documentation should include:

· An inventory and appraisal

· An allocation agreement

· New title documents for real property (showing that the property is either in the A or B trust)

- The title should also be changed on the various trust accounts (showing that these accounts are either in the A or the B trust).

- At the death of the first spouse, a 706 estate tax return should be prepared and filed to establish the B trust every year until the death of the surviving spouse.

If the above documentation is not carried out, it could have serious tax consequences for the family. For example, without it, the IRS may feel that the surviving spouse has not abided by an identifiable standard and spent indiscriminately from Trust B. It could then decide that the surviving spouse has a general power of appointment over that trust. If so, the IRS would consider the Trust B assets as part of the surviving spouse's estate, and none of those assets could bypass the estate tax. Instead, they would be subject to the estate tax on death of the surviving spouse. It is important to not only establish the AB trust properly up-front, but to administer it correctly on the death of the first spouse. The successor trustee is responsible for filing any required federal and state estate tax returns.

Responsibilities and Duties for AB Disclaimer Trusts

With these trusts, Trust A is created only when the surviving spouse decides to disclaim trust property. In that event, there is not a requirement for a new trust document, but new schedules should be prepared listing the property in both Trust A and B. As with the AB trust, the schedules should be prepared to meet IRS expectations. As trustee, the surviving spouse needs to first distribute any trust property the deceased spouse left to specific beneficiaries and then must maintain the remainder of the property in ongoing Trust A. If a child's trust is involved, the successor trustee must manage the property within that trust. The successor trustee is also responsible for filing any required federal and state estate tax returns.

12
What Other Methods of Probate Avoidance Are There?

A living trust is a large part of estate planning, but it is not the only part. A will is a necessity, especially if you are in a state where you cannot use a living trust to appoint a personal guardian to care for minor children. A will is also necessary for any property you have not transferred to your living trust. If you decide you want to disinherit a spouse or a child, you need to make that decision clear in your will. Beyond the living trust, there are several methods of probate avoidance that may be appropriate for your needs. You can combine these methods with the living trust to create the best possible mix for protecting your assets from probate. This chapter covers the common methods of probate avoidance.

Pay-on-Death (POD) Financial Accounts

This is a common methods of avoiding probate. It is easy and quick to set up. POD accounts are used mainly for bank accounts (checking, savings, and certificate of deposit accounts). It is also possible to register ownership of government securities (bonds, Treasury bills, and Treasury notes) so you can name a beneficiary for those items. To set up a POD account, all you need to do is designate beneficiaries on a form provided by your financial institution. Your beneficiaries will receive the monies upon your death. For example, a savings account might be set up in the following way:

> Kim opens a saving account with his bank and names Brook as his POD beneficiary. When Kim dies, all monies in the account go to Brook.
>
> During Kim's lifetime, Brook has no right to the money in the savings account. Kim can withdraw the money or close the account as he wishes. He also has the option of changing the beneficiary. Upon Kim's death, the beneficiary can claim the monies through a simple process of showing the death certificate and personal identification to bank officials.

These types of financial accounts can be temporarily frozen upon your death. This occurs when your state levies estate taxes. If this is the case, the state releases the money to your beneficiaries after they confirm your estate has sufficient funds to pay the taxes. Check with your bank or the appropriate governmental office to find out if estate taxes are levied in your state. If they are, be sure to let your beneficiaries know so they are prepared to face the aggravation.

States may also stipulate that a POD account is not effective unless you have notified the beneficiaries that the account has been set up. You will need to check with your bank to see if this rule is in effect in your area.

Transfer-on-Death (TOD) Registration for Stocks and Bonds

Depending on the state you live in, it should be possible to register your securities in a transfer-on-death form. These securities include individual stocks, bonds, brokerage accounts, and mutual funds. As of this writing, the only states that do not allow this action are New York, North Carolina, and Texas. The process is similar to a POD bank account. When you register your ownership with the stockbroker (or the company itself), you make a request to take ownership on a form that designates a beneficiary. When your ownership papers are issued, they will show your name and the name of your beneficiary. As with a POD account, the beneficiary has no rights to the securities while you are alive. Upon your death, your beneficiary can claim the securities without probate by simply providing the death certificate and identification to the broker or other appropriate agent.

Individual Retirement Accounts (IRAs and 401(k))

When opening a retirement account, you will be asked to name a beneficiary for that account. After you die, the funds in the account do not have to go through probate but can be claimed directly by the beneficiary from the account custodian. If you are single, you can choose whomever you want as the beneficiary. However, if you are married, your spouse may have rights to the money.

- With a 401(k) account, your spouse is entitled to inherit the money unless he or she agrees, in writing, to the choice of another beneficiary.

When you live in a community property state, the odds are good that your spouse owns half the funds in your retirement account. Community property states include Arizona, California, Idaho, Louisiana, New Mexico, Nevada, Texas, Washington, and Wisconsin. In Alaska, you and your spouse have the option of signing an agreement that designates your property as community property. If any of the money you contributed to the retirement account was earned while you were married, that money remains community property, so your spouse owns half.

Life Insurance

Life insurance can be an excellent method of providing your beneficiaries with fast cash for debts, living expenses, and in the case of large estates, taxes on those estates. The proceeds from life insurance do not go through probate because the beneficiary is named in the policy itself and not in your will. This is not the case when you have named your estate as the beneficiary, which may be done if the estate needs quick cash to pay debts and taxes.

Joint Tenancy

Joint tenancy is a method by which two or more people can hold title to property they own together, and it is available in nearly all states. By law, all joint tenants must own equal shares of the property. It is a common and effective way to transfer certain types of property. It is also an easy way to avoid probate when the first owner dies. You normally do not have to prepare and submit any additional documents. All that needs to be done is for you to state how you hold title on the papers that show your ownership (for example, a real estate deed, car title, or bank account information). Your state may require additional paperwork. The surviving owner automatically gets total ownership of the property called "joint tenancy with right of survivorship." With this arrangement you cannot leave your share of property to anyone other than the surviving joint tenants.

Joint tenancy is a good choice for probate avoidance and estate planning when couples acquire real estate or other property together because probate is avoided when the first owner dies. A second benefit comes when you transfer the property to your living trust, even when you already own it in joint tenancy, because you create the option to name an alternate beneficiary. This cannot be done in a joint trust alone. This allows you to name someone to inherit the property in the event your first beneficiary (your spouse) does not survive you. Another benefit is that you will avoid probate when both the first spouse and the second spouse die. In the case of joint tenancy, probate is avoided only when the first spouse dies.

When you are older, joint tenancy may not be a good choice for estate planning. It can create several problems for you. First, there is no way to change your mind. Once there is joint tenancy, the co-owner gets half ownership, and you cannot take back that right. This can create problems. A good example is half-ownership of a particular property. Your co-owner can do what he or she likes with his or her share of that property. This means they can sell it or mortgage it. This can create problems when creditors are involved. Here is an example:

Donna signs a deed for a piece of property. She lists her daughter Corinne as co-owner to avoid probate at Donna's death. Corrine starts a business, which does not do well. She ends up owing her creditors a significant amount of money. The creditors sue her to get the half-interest in the property and to get at least part of their money back. If they succeed, then the property will be sold. Donna would get her half of the value of the property, and the creditors would get the other half.

A second potential problem with joint tenancy lies in the matter of incapacity. If one joint tenant is incapacitated and is incapable of making decisions, the other owner(s) need to get legal authority to sell or mortgage the property. Depending on what state you are in, this may mean going to court to get a conservator appointed to manage the afflicted co-owner's affairs. However, this problem can be dealt with (in part) by having the joint tenant sign a "Durable Power of Attorney" document. This gives a selected person the authority to manage his or her affairs in the case of incapacity.

A third potential problem with joint tenancy is that you may have to file a gift tax return. This occurs when the value of the interest you give to a new co-owner (except for your spouse) exceeds $12,000 in one year. You are then required to file a gift tax return with the IRS. There is an exception, however. If two or more people open a joint tenancy bank account, but if one person puts in most or all of the money, then no gift tax is levied against that person. When a joint tenant who has contributed little or nothing to the account withdraws money from that account, then a taxable gift may be made. No tax is due, however, until you leave or give away a large amount (currently more than $1 million) in taxable gifts.

A fourth problem with joint tenancy is the possibility of disputes after your death. A common mistake older people may make is the addition of a joint tenant to their bank checking and savings accounts. This may be done to get the assistance of someone to handle the deposit of checks and bill payments. This works fine while the original owner lives. But after he or she dies, it is then possible the co-owner may stake a lay claim to the remaining funds, because it was the intention of the deceased person to bequeath it to them. Such a claim may be true, but after the original owner is dead, there is no way to learn the truth. If your intention is to give someone authority and allow them to use your money on your behalf, use a power of attorney.

A fifth potential problem with joint tenancy is that an income tax break could be missed by the surviving spouse. This may occur when you are both joint tenants on property you own separately. The IRS rule is: A surviving spouse gets a stepped-up tax basis only for the 50 percent of the property owned by the deceased spouse. When the property is sold, the tax basis is the amount from which taxable profit is figured. This may not be a problem if you live in a community property state. If the joint tenancy property is community property, then it will still qualify for a stepped-up tax basis. This is the case if the surviving spouse can prove to the IRS that it was indeed community property. However, the IRS assumes that property held in joint tenancy is not community property, so you will have to be able to provide proof that it is such. When the property is later sold, this means a higher tax if the property has appreciated in value after the joint tenancy was created but before the first spouse died.

Tenancy by the Entirety

This is similar to joint tenancy, but it is only available to married couples (or same-sex couples in Hawaii and Vermont who have registered with those states). As of this writing, tenancy by the entirety is limited to these states:

Alaska	Maryland	Oregon*
Arkansas	Massachusetts	Pennsylvania
Delaware	Michigan*	Rhode Island
District of Columbia	Mississippi	Tennessee
Florida	Missouri	Vermont
Hawaii	New York*	Virginia
Illinois*	North Carolina*	Wyoming
Indiana	Ohio**	
Kentucky*	Oklahoma	

Allowed for real estate only.
** Only if created before April 4, 1985.*

Here is how tenancy by the entirety works: When property is held in this form of tenancy, neither spouse is able to transfer their half of the property alone. They cannot do this while alive or by will or trust. This means that a living spouse needs to get the other spouse's consent to transfer the property (unlike joint tenancy, in which a joint tenant has the option of transferring his or her share to someone else during his or her lifetime). For example, if Jim and Mary hold title to an investment property in tenancy by the entirety and Jim wants to sell, he has to get Mary's consent and her signature on the deed to that property. At death, tenancy by the entirety property has to go to the surviving spouse.

Community Property with Right of Survivorship

This is a probate-avoidance option in several states, such as Alaska, Arizona, California, Nevada, and Wisconsin. If you register with these states as domestic partners and live or own property in them, then you and your spouse can hold title to your community property "with right of survivorship." This means that when one spouse dies, the other one owns all the property by default. The advantage of this option is the property does not need to go through probate upon the death of one spouse. Wisconsin adds another benefit. It has a "marital property agreement." In this agreement, the couple can name a beneficiary to inherit their property without need of probate. It can be a person, a trust, or other entity.

Transfer-on-Death (TOD) Deeds

This is a deed that is effective only at death and is only available in the following states: Arizona, Arkansas, Colorado, Kansas, Ohio, Missouri, Nevada, New Mexico, and Wisconsin. Such deeds need to be titled transfer-on-death or TOD. They need to be signed, notarized, and recorded in the appropriate property records office.

Gifts

There is a simple premise behind giving gifts: if you do not own it when you die, then probate is not required on those gifts. Therefore, smaller amounts of property in your estate mean less will go through probate upon your death, which then lowers probate costs. Tax-exempt gifts are a good idea if you want to reduce federal estate taxes on your estate after your death.

Small Estates — Simplified Procedures

A number of states have attempted to modify or eliminate the costly aspects of probate. They offer simplified alternatives for small estates. These alternatives include the following:

- **Claiming Property with Affidavits — No Court Required**. Your heirs may be able to entirely escape probate if the total value of all the personal property (except for real estate) in your estate is less than a specified amount. This amount varies by state. For example, the limit in California is $100,000, while Wyoming has a limit of $150,000. When an estate is qualified, the person inheriting that estate can write a short document that he or she is entitled to the stated properties under a will or state law. This document is called an "affidavit" and must be signed under oath. Upon receipt of the affidavit and the death certificate, the person or institution holding the property will release the properties or monies.

- **Leaving Property to the Surviving Spouse — No Court Required**. This may be an option in your state. With this option, no probate is necessary if the surviving spouse inherits less than a specified amount of property.

- **Simplified Probate Court Procedures**. In states that

have simplified probate, this process may be a good choice for your heirs. They may be able to settle your estate without a lawyer, which saves money and time. However, to use the simplified probate process, the value of your estate cannot exceed the maximum amount set by state law. There are exceptions, so it pays to learn about your state's specific procedures.

The key is to understand each of these probate-avoidance options thoroughly and to know the "nuts and bolts" of the state laws governing these options. Knowledge is power in terms of saving your beneficiaries time, money, and trouble.

13
Do I Still Need a Will If I Have a Living Trust?

The answer is a definite yes. There are several reasons for preparing a will.

1. You cannot name a personal guardian for young children in a living trust (in many states) — it has to be done through a will. A will is a good choice for young couples with children who do not have much property; it is simpler and less expensive.

2. You can select a beneficiary for newly acquired property. In the event of receiving an unexpected inheritance or gift, you may not have the time to transfer that property to your trust. If that happens and you do not have a will, the property would go to your closest relatives under your state's "intestate succession" laws. You may not want it to go to those individuals.

3. With a will you can make sure your property goes to the intended beneficiaries in case you have not planned and set into effect probate-avoidance devices.

4. You can give away property left to you that is still in probate. For example, assume Uncle Harold left you real estate in his will, but it ended up embroiled in probate proceedings. You do not have title to that property, so you have no legal right to transfer it. If you die without listing that property in your will, it may be lost. However, if it is named in your will that Uncle Harold's real estate will go to your residual beneficiary after it is released by the probate court, it may not be lost.

5. You can name an executor and alternate executor. This is the person with the legal authority to supervise distribution of the property left by your will. The executor also has the legal authority to represent your estate in probate court. An executor is a reassurance to banks and other financial institutions, because they are not always comfortable with living trusts. You have the right to name the same person as the successor trustee in your living trust and as executor of your will.

6. Though remote, there is a chance of the simultaneous death of married partners. Wills assume that one partner will die before the other. For example, in a car accident resulting in simultaneous deaths it can be impossible to determine who died first. This confusion can be prevented by inserting a clause into the will that assumes the writer of the will is presumed to have outlived the other spouse. When each marriage partner has a will, the wills are interpreted independently from the other.

Before getting into the type of will of particular relevance to trusts — the pour-over will — here is important information on basic forms of wills that will be helpful to you.

The Basics of Wills

A will is a method of stating how you want your property disposed of at death. It can be a written or oral communication. Wills come in the following forms:

- **Self-proving Will** — A common type, this is a written will that has been witnessed and signed with all the formalities required by state law.

- **Holographic Will** — This is a handwritten will made without the presence of witnesses. It must be written and cannot be typed or computer-generated. It must also be signed and dated. These wills may used in situations in which a person has minimal estate issues that can arise after death. A self-proving will may be a better choice in certain circumstances, but a holographic will has more validity than an oral will.

- **Oral Will** — As the name indicates, the person communicates or dictates his or her wishes orally. Oral wills may not be considered valid because of the written requirements dictated by state laws. However, they are recognized in specific, emergency situations such as the imminent danger of death or by soldiers during active service, when there is no chance to prepare a written will or to have it properly executed. Particularly in the case of estates, you do not want an oral will because it can be contested easily.

Wills have certain basic requirements.

- You have to be of sound mind and at least 18 years old. You have to know what a will is and understand what it does.

- You have to specifically state the document is your will and then sign and date it.

- The signing must be "attested to" (signed) by a specific number of witnesses. The number depends on the laws of the state where you reside. Your state may require the witnesses be unrelated to you.

- There must be a provision that appoints a guardian for minor children, lists the individuals who inherit specific items, and states what happens to the remaining property not specifically listed in the will.

- An executor must be appointed. This person is responsible for proper distribution of property and for ensuring all debts and taxes are paid.

Different types of wills relate specifically to people with living trusts.

Pour-Over Wills

A pour-over will gets its name from the fact that it takes all the property not transferred to your living trust and upon your death "pours it over" to that trust. It provides you with legal backup in case you accidentally leave property outside your trust; it is a catchall device. A pour-over will is a simple legal document that does the following:

1. It identifies the individual by name.

2. It pours into the living trust any personal or household items left outside the trust.

3. It pours any real assets left outside the trust into that trust.

4. It names the executor and assigns the authority to take pour-over assets through probate.

Any pour-over assets must first go through probate — a good reason to make sure all your valuable assets are in your living trust.

Make sure the pour-over will and living trust mesh well. You do not want conflicting provisions that can create confusion or disputes among beneficiaries. For example, do not leave the same property in your living trust and in your pour-over will. This will create confusion and may also cause probate to rear its ugly head. A good way to minimize or eliminate any potential problems is to name the same person to be executor of your will and the successor trustee of your living trust. The exception involves a basic shared trust or AB Trust. In those cases, it is likely you will name your spouse the executor of your will but not as successor trustee. The successor trustee assumes responsibility only after both spouses are deceased. It is therefore possible the surviving spouse may want to revise the pour-over will after the first spouse's death to name a successor trustee to be executor.

A good example of a pour-over will can be found at **www. tax-business.com/Will.pdf.** If you review this example, you will see it is written in terms of a married couple. The term used is "wife" since John Wannabe is the husband. If it were the wife's will, then she would refer to her "husband." Mr. Wannabe's city, state, and county are indicated in the first line of the will's main body. In this particular will, Mr. Wannabe names his wife Mary as "personal representative" of his last will and testament. His brother Ted is named as "successor personal representative." Mr. Wannabe then gives his wife the authority to pay any remaining debts and lists all her powers under Section III. In the next section, he lists his sister as guardian of his minor children if his wife does not survive him. The "simultaneous death" clause noted earlier in this book is included next, and then in the next section Mr. Wannabe bequeaths all his "tangible personal property" to his wife. He does not list specifics, just "household effects and goods, furniture, automobiles, works of art, books, clothing, and all other personal effects of like nature."

There is no need to get more specific than this in your pour-over will. In Section VII, Mr. Wannabe bequeaths the "residue of estate" to "that corporation or person" serving as trustee of the "John Wannabe Living Trust." This is the section that "pours" the specified property over into a trust. As the remainder of the document indicates, you need witnesses to your signature and to the notarization of your will. The number of witnesses required varies by state, but three signatures is a good idea because this provides more proof that your signature is valid if it becomes an issue during probate. Here are the qualifications for witnesses:

- They must be adults (18 or over) and of sound mind.

- They must be people who will not inherit under the will. This includes individuals who might inherit a gift through your will, including alternate residuary beneficiaries. However, someone who will receive property only through your living trust is considered a valid witness.

- They should be individuals who are easy to locate in the event of your death. You should choose people who are not prone to move around and who are younger than you are.

It is important to write your pour-over will carefully. You should write an initial draft, leave it alone for a day or two, and then revise it and include what you missed in the first draft. After you have decided on a final form for your will, key it into a word processing program and print it out. Do not make any alterations or write on the form, as this could invalidate the will. Make your will clean, uncomplicated, and easy for a judge and other individuals to read. Do not sign or date your will yet, as this needs to be done in front of witnesses.

14
How Do I Develop an Estate Plan?

The previous chapters in this book have dealt with the various forms of living trusts, but they are only one part of an estate plan. This is where many people stumble. They procrastinate for various reasons — not wanting to think about their eventual death or simply avoiding paperwork. This is a negative attitude that should be replaced with a positive one. The point of estate planning is not to provide for the dead but to provide for the living — your beneficiaries. You want the best possible future for them, so the investment of time and money can give them a prosperous future. Here is the difference between having an estate plan and not having one:

ESTATE PLAN

- You decide who receives your assets or a share of them.
- You decide how and when the assets are received by your beneficiaries.
- You decide who will be the administrator/manager of your estate (executor, trustee).
- You can reduce estate taxes and administrative expenses.
- You can select a guardian for your child.
- You can provide for the orderly continuance or sale of a family business.

NO ESTATE PLAN

- State laws determine who inherits your assets; they could pass assets to a relative you never intended to have any part of your estate.

- The law sets the terms and timing of the estate disposition. It is possible your children could be left in complete control of a large estate and end up squandering it.

- The court appoints estate administrators, and these administrators' ideas may not be the same as yours in terms of disposition of assets.

- In many cases, costs are greater because of required administrative expenses and unnecessary taxes.

- The court appoints a guardian for your child.

- An untimely forced sale may result in financial losses, and family hardships may result. The IRS expects to be paid estate taxes nine (9) months after date of death.

It is critical to properly plan your estate. To do that, you have to ask yourself these basic questions.

Who Do You Want to Inherit Your Assets?

This is a personal and difficult decision. You will need to ask yourself more questions:

· If married, "What do I want to provide for my spouse?"

· If you have children, "Should my children share equally in my inheritance?" For example, one of your children may have special needs and may need a greater amount than the others.

· If you have grandchildren, "Do I want to name my grandchildren (or others) as beneficiaries?"

What Assets Should My Beneficiaries Inherit?

The division of assets will have to be considered. How they are allocated will depend on the nature of those assets. For example, assume you own closely-held business stock and some of your children are involved in the business. Should that stock pass only to those children who are active in your business? Or should you compensate non-active children with assets of comparable value? Or perhaps you own rental properties. If that is the case, should all beneficiaries inherit them or is one person better at managing property and therefore a more suitable beneficiary?

When Should Your Assets Be Inherited by the Beneficiaries?

To answer this question, you need to consider the age and maturity level of your beneficiaries. This leads to other questions. For example, do you want some assets distributed right away after your death to mature beneficiaries or will you need to place those assets in a trust with distributions made over a number of years as beneficiaries mature? You will also need to consider the size of your estate. It is not unusual to hear of young beneficiaries receiving substantial amounts of money and running through their estate assets in short order because of their immaturity. If you have such beneficiaries, you may want to distribute your assets to them over a number of years.

You may also ask yourself, "Should I start a gift program for my beneficiaries?" This will give you tax benefits as well as psychological benefits for the beneficiary; for example, if you have a family business and a child active in that business, a gift of company stock can increase that child's motivation to make sure the company grows. Gifts can provide a training time during which he or she can be taught how to manage assets carefully and prudently.

The Will

Another vital part of your estate plan is your will. It is the primary document for transferring your wealth upon your death. If you die without a will (intestate), you place the disposition of your assets in the hands of state law. In that case, the state will provide a will for you when you die; this situation can set up all kinds of costly complications and take a long time. There is no room to cover all aspects of a will in this chapter, but here are major provisions a will should include:

- **A trust creation** — A will is limited to the disposition of your estate. You must include instructions for the creation of trusts if you desire longer-term goals such as funding a child's education. One important aspect to consider in any trust is selecting your trustee.

- **A children's guardian** — In case you and your spouse both die, your will should name a guardian for your minor children. Take time deciding who should be your children's guardian. You should choose someone you can trust and who has similar beliefs on raising children. Before you name this person in the will, it is important to make sure the person you choose is willing to accept the responsibility.

· **Selecting an executor and trustee(s)** — After your death, the executor is your personal representative and has major responsibilities including the payment of estate expenses and any debts.

An executor can be either an individual or a corporate (for example, bank) executor. The choice depends on the complexity of your estate and your individual preference. You can also opt to use both and name them as co-executors. There are advantages to each:

Corporate Executor/Trustee Advantages
1. Specialists in the handling of estates and trusts
2. No emotional involvement
3. Impartiality
4. Never moves, goes on vacation
5. Never dies or becomes ill
Individual Executor/Trustee Advantages
1. Familiarity with family and its specific needs
2. Possible lower costs

Whether you choose an individual or corporate executor, be sure to take the following considerations into account:

· The executor should be willing to serve. His or her duties are not necessarily easy, and not everyone will want the job.

· Name an alternate executor in the will in the event the primary executor is unable or unwilling to serve in that capacity.

· Establish that there is no conflict of interest on the part of the executor. For example, if you run a co-owned business, it may not be a good idea to name the co-owner as executor. His or her ideas may have different goals for the business than your beneficiaries have, and that could lead to costly conflict.

Here are additional recommendations in relation to wills and trusts. These suggestions, if followed, can add to your peace of mind about estate planning matters:

· Write a post-mortem letter of instructions to your spouse and beneficiaries. The letter should specify your funeral wishes. It should also list all your financial accounts. In addition, the letter should tell your heirs the location of your will, tax returns, and essential documents. This prevents waste of estate assets on avoidable taxes and administrative costs.

· Create a durable power of attorney. This allows an appointed person to make financial decisions on your behalf if you or your spouse suffers incapacitation. It is also a good idea to have a living will that specifies your wishes concerning life-prolonging medical procedures. You should also have a health-care power of attorney, naming somebody to make medical decisions if you are incapacitated. As we saw with the Terri Schiavo case in 2005, it can be a gut-wrenching experience on a personal and national level. Ms. Schiavo was in a persistent vegetative state for 15 years. Her husband wanted to remove her feeding tube so she could die in peace as he said she had verbally directed; her parents opposed the move saying that as a devout Roman Catholic she would be opposed to what they considered euthanasia. Since there was no living will, a legal battle erupted involving the courts, the Florida state legislature, and even Congress. The situation could have been avoided with a health care directive and a living will. A health care directive can have many different names depending on the state; Advance Health Care Directive, Declaration Regarding Health Care, Designation of Health Care Surrogate, Directive to Physicians, Do Not Resuscitate, Medical Directive, and Patient Advocate Designation are all terms for a health care directive. An example of a combined health-care power of attorney and living will is provided in the Appendix.

· Vacation property located in another state should be placed in a revocable living trust so that your estate will not end up going through probate in two states. Check with your attorney to make sure this is a good idea under your state's laws.

· If you have a large estate, give away money to your heirs now. You can give $11,000 per year ($22,000 per married couple), to each donee (with no limit on the number of donees) without incurring gift tax liability.

Update your estate plan as needed so that it will be implemented exactly in the way you wish. You should update our estate plan when the following events occur:

- Births

- Deaths

- Marriages

- Divorces

- A significant increase or decrease in the value of your estate

- A change in tax laws

- A move to another state

- Your business or career changes

After you have answered the questions posed near the beginning of this chapter, you will be ready to draw up the living trust. If you are going to use a professional (attorney or estate-planning specialist), you will have to provide them with specific information and documents such as:

- Personal information (names of children and dates of birth, names of parents and dates of birth, and any other pertinent personal details)

- Names of individuals you have chosen as trustees, executors and guardians

- Information regarding your desired allocation of assets

- Copies of deeds (real estate, trust)

- Separate property agreements

- Business papers

- Will of deceased spouse

Be sure to provide information about grant deeds for all real estate properties you own, as they need to be transferred into the living trust. You should have your attorney prepare and file these documents unless you are well-versed in this field. Provide deed copies to the professional, and he or she will draw up new deeds at the same time your living trust is created. Be sure to include the correct assessor's parcel number and the property address with each deed to make sure the correct property is recorded. Simple mistakes or omissions can create trouble down the road, so double check all information from the beginning. If you are holding first or second trust deeds on the property of other people, these are also assets that must be transferred in the living trust so provide copies of those to the professional you are working with. In terms of business papers (partnerships, sole proprietorships, or other business organizations), provide copies of those as well. Request a Notice of Assignment, Bill of Sale, or Letter of Transfer so your interest in the business can be transferred into the trust. See the Appendix for an example of a Notice of Assignment. Do not forget to provide a list of any assets you want designated as separate property.

Also be sure to provide a copy of your deceased spouse's will if you are a widow or widower so everything can be covered by the attorney or estate-planner.

15
How Do I Settle a Living Trust?

The subject of this book has been how to set up and manage living trusts, but is possible you may have to deal with the settlement of a living trust either as a beneficiary or a successor trustee. The death of a loved one is a sad and stressful event, and settlement procedures are the last thing on anyone's mind. The information in this chapter should make the settlement process easier should you ever face such a situation.

As a beneficiary, your role in the settlement process is relatively simple. You wait to be contacted by the successor trustee and then receive your portion of the settlement. On the other hand, if you are the successor trustee (and/or surviving spouse), then your settlement responsibilities fall into four basic areas:

- Pay debts as specified in trust

- Collect debts

- Hire attorney if needed

· Contact inheritors and distribute assets

To carry out the above responsibilities, you will need to find and collect information. To find that information you may have to research:

· Charge accounts

· Charitable contributions

· Hospital and medical expenses

· Insurance policies and dividends

· Investments (CDs, IRAs, 401(k) accounts)

· Mortgages and rents for properties owned

· Pension benefits

· Safe deposit box

· Stock dividend and bond interest payments

· Social Security

· Taxes and tax refunds

· Utility payments

· Veterans benefits

You will need to follow specific guidelines if you are the successor trustee. These are outlined in the following pages.

Guideline 1: Make Arrangements for the Appropriate Funeral/Memorial Services

This may sound like an obvious step, and it may be a straight-forward one. However, although the deceased may leave specific funeral arrangement instructions (for example, cremation, burial, and other arrangements) in his or her will, members of the family may have other ideas. The surviving spouse may be opposed to cremation on religious grounds and try to fight this provision in the living trust. This can create conflict with other family members who want to see the trust provision carried out exactly as planned by the deceased. These situations are rare, but they can occur. As successor trustee you should try to carry out the deceased's wishes as stipulated in the will and/or living trust.

To make it easier for the funeral home to complete the death certificate, you should have personal information on the deceased on hand. This includes the deceased's full name, date of birth, place of birth, father's full name and place of birth, mother's full name (including maiden name) and place of birth, and marriage date and location.

Guideline 2: Collect the Necessary Documentation

Locate the deceased's fully executed copy of the living trust. The deceased should have kept two copies in separate locations to guard against loss or destruction of one. If the deceased has a safe deposit box, be sure to check its contents. This should be done before funeral arrangements are made in case there

THE COMPLETE GUIDE TO CREATING YOUR OWN LIVING TRUST

have been changes related to those arrangements. In terms of the funeral costs and any last illness costs, keep detailed records . These can be deducted on the deceased person's 1040 individual income tax return or on the 706 federal estate tax return. Either form may be used.

Guideline 3: Contact the Appropriate People, Agencies, and Institutions

As successor trustee, you are responsible for contacting the inheritors of the estate, but there are also specific agencies and institutions you may need to get in touch with to inform them of the death of the person. These may include:

Social Security Administration (SSA)

If the deceased was a recipient of Social Security benefits, notify the Social Security Administration (SSA) that the person has passed away. Since it will take time for this information to pass through the federal bureaucracy, Social Security checks may continue to be deposited into the deceased's bank account. Be sure to retain this money in his or her bank account; eventually the SSA will ask for a refund of all payments made after death.

The surviving spouse is also eligible for survivor benefits from the SSA. These benefits commence on the date and month in which the spouse died. The Social Security Administration will not initiate these benefits without proof of the marriage. As successor trustee you will need to ask the surviving spouse to provide the marriage certificate to establish eligibility. If the surviving spouse has Medicare eligibility, those medical benefits will continue. In addition, the SSA has a provision for a $255 burial benefit; make sure the surviving spouse receives it.

Former Employer(s)

If the deceased received a pension from former employers, it will be necessary for you to contact these companies to inform them of the death and to determine what employee benefits are being provided. Contact the Human Resources department to determine those benefits, which may include insurance policies, stock options, and pension and retirement programs.

Military Retirement Benefits

If the deceased was a member of the armed forces, contact the local Department of Veterans Affairs to notify them of the individual's death and also to inform them of the surviving spouse who is eligible for survivor's benefits and medical benefits. The benefits are too numerous to list in their entirety here, but they fall into the following categories:

· Dependency Indemnity Compensation (DIC)

· Death pension

· Survivors' and Dependents' Educational Assistance (DEA)

· Home Loan Guaranty

- Medical – CHAMPVA

- Bereavement Counseling

- Specialized Vocational Counseling

- VA Life Insurance

- Financial Counseling

- Burial Benefits

- Burial Flags

- Related Benefits

- TRICARE Retiree Dental Program

- Social Security Administration

- Civil Service Preference

- Commissary and Exchange Privileges

- Montgomery GI Bill Death Benefit

- Death Gratuity

- Military Records and Medals

- Burial at Arlington National Cemetery

- Internal Revenue Service information

Insurance Policies and Annuities

If the deceased person had insurance policies or annuities in force, find the paperwork and then notify the companies of the death. They will require certified copies of the death certificate, and may not accept photocopies because of the potential for fraud. Be sure to order several certified death certificates right away. This saves time, aggravation, and makes settlement much easier. For example, each asset in a trust normally requires one death certificate. If you have to order additional certificate copies, this could take anywhere from a month to six weeks depending on the efficiency of the local government agency. Copies will be required by insurance agencies, annuity providers, IRA retirement plans, pension providers, and others so it is much easier to have enough death certificate copies on hand.

Guideline 4: Take Care of Other Important Items

If you are the surviving spouse and the successor trustee, grief may cause you to forget the basics of everyday finance. While they may not seem important at the moment, neglecting them can cause problems. For example, failing to make a payment and letting something like your homeowner's insurance policies lapse can be catastrophic financially if fire or damage occurs. It is important to keep them up to date. The same is true for monthly bills — especially the mortgage payments. Taxes on the real estate property in the trust assets must be paid as well. They will need to be accounted for on the survivor's Form 1040 individual income tax return by the end of year. Also be sure to check on credit cards; they will need to be canceled or transferred into the name of the surviving spouse.

Debts

Debts fall into two categories — those owed to the estate and those owed to creditors. If debts are owed to the estate, determine what they are and collect them before distributing assets from the trust. If debts are owed by the estate, pay them. If the debts are mortgages or notes, continue making the monthly payments as this form of debt does not become due upon death.

Inventory of Trust Assets

This inventory should be of "real" assets (not personal effects) such as real estate, checking accounts, stocks, bonds, and savings accounts. The important part of this process is to determine the title(s) in which all these assets are held. The inventory is important in determining the amount of inheritance taxes (if any) due. It also ensures equitable distribution of assets to beneficiaries.

Notice to Creditors

Filing a notice to creditors is normally a standard practice for probate, but it can also be a good idea to file one in conjunction with a living trust to eliminate nuisance claims that may arise. There is a cut-off period in which creditors can file claims against an estate. After that they lose their right to file such claims and cannot collect monies owed to them. Your particular state may not have a regulatory function regarding notification of creditors in conjunction with living trusts, but a filing action establishes precedent for you, which may be useful in potential legal actions against the estate. It also has the effect of surfacing both legitimate and frivolous legal claims so you can deal with them quickly and not be unpleasantly surprised later. If the claims are legitimate, you can pay them and get them out of the way. If they are illegitimate, hopefully the living trust has been worded in such a way that it allows trustees to take the assets in question out of the trust and through the probate process. The probate court is responsible for preserving the assets of an estate, and the court will take a dim view of any spurious claims and dismiss them. If you file a notice to creditors, do not distribute any trust assets until after the notification period has expired.

Inheritance Taxes

f you live in a state in which inheritance taxes are due, they must be paid in cash within nine months of the deceased's death. Do not delay and run up against or past the deadline. The Internal Revenue Service is not a forgiving agency when taxes are not paid.

Guideline 5: Determine the Value of Assets in the Trust

Determination of trust assets value is a vital step because it directly affects settlement in three ways:

· It determines whether or not federal estate taxes are due.

THE COMPLETE GUIDE TO CREATING YOUR OWN LIVING TRUST

· It affects apportionment of assets into the survivor's A trust and the decedent's B trust and/or a C trust (upon the death of the first spouse).

· It allows for equitable distribution of assets (as specified in the living trust) to the beneficiaries.

It is in your interest to get the estate assets valued and distributed within a reasonable amount of time. Timely action will prevent you from getting unnecessarily caught up in the machinery of federal bureaucracy. For example, if the value of estate assets appreciates from the date of death and the time of valuation, you may be setting yourself up for a challenge from the IRS; the agency could decide you are undervaluing the estate assets and demand additional taxes.

Get a written valuation of trust assets — all real assets that are held in title by the decedent. You can do this either as of the date of death or six months later. However, if you use the six-month period, be sure to include the entire estate in the re-valuation. This means the latest value of all assets must be accounted for. A potential negative of using the six-month period is that it may trigger an IRS audit since the agency considers this period a "red flag." Written valuation of trust assets means you must obtain specific valuation of each asset. Here is information on how many of the types of assets need to be handled.

Bank and Credit Union Accounts

Hopefully the decedent clearly indicated these items within the trust documents and provided the names, addresses, and account numbers of the specific financial institutions in their living trust. The IRS wants clear documentation, and it is up to you to provide it. If it is not obvious where the decedent has placed his or her assets, you will have to do a bit of detective work to find out where they are located. These assets could include checking accounts, savings accounts, CDs, money market accounts, a safety deposit box, and others. After you have identified the various institutions, you need to obtain a written valuation of the accounts at the time of death. It may be as easy as reading the next statements that arrive in the mail, or it may require contacting the institutions directly. In the case of a securities portfolio, you may be able to access the account online and get a current value.

Stocks, Bonds, and Mutual Funds

If securities were included in the assets of the living trust, you can get the value of these securities from the stock market's closing value on the date of death or six months later. The simplest method to determine valuation is to contact the brokerage with which the decedent had an account and request written documentation. Another method is to use the Internet to access portfolio prices. If you do this, print out the information and save it as proof for the IRS.

Annuities

To determine the valuation of any annuity included in the assets of the living trust, contact a financial advisor or insurance company and ask them to determine the accumulated value of the annuity or of the death benefit (if the deceased was the annuitant — the person who is entitled to receive benefits from the annuity. In the latter case, the institution providing the annuity will require a certified copy of the death certificate to provide the proceeds of the death benefit.

Insurance Policies

Locate all insurance policies and identify them clearly in the estate's assets. If the decedent was named as the insured on one or more policies, you will need to notify the companies of the death and indicate that you wish to be paid the benefit. Again, you will need to provide a certified copy of the death certificate for each policy paying a benefit. If there are insurance policies on the surviving spouse's life, you will need to identify the cash value of each policy because the cash value must be included in the estate's value. To get the value(s), contact the insurance companies and request that they provide you with the cash value in the survivor's policy as of the date of death of the first spouse. However, if the insurance policies were previously placed in an insurance trust, the policies are excluded from the estate. In this situation, they are excluded when figuring the estate's value for estate tax or inheritance tax purposes.

Real Estate

To properly value real estate in the estate, you will need to engage the services of a professional real estate appraiser as quickly as possible after the death of the decedent (preferably within the first month). Appraisers' fees will vary according to the state and the size of the estate; these fees may fall in a range from $200 to $1,500. This is money well-invested, particularly if the real estate value has appreciated since it was purchased. The surviving spouse or the beneficiaries can take advantage of stepped-up valuation to reduce or eliminate future capital gains taxes at the eventual sale of the real estate.

You may want to get appraisals from two different companies and then average the difference between the two if they are reasonably close in their valuations. If they are far apart you will need a third appraisal. This establishes proof for the IRS that the appraisals are realistic. Do not forget to ask the appraisers to include comparable information to support their valuations. "Comparables" refers to the prices of similar pieces of real estate within a defined radius in the neighborhood. All information should be provided in writing, and you should have at least two copies of these appraisals in two separate places for safekeeping. An attorney may recommend the real estate in the decedent's B trust and/or C trust be "re-titled." However, Henry W. Abts III, in his book *How to Settle Your Living Trust* (1999), says this approach is unnecessary and potentially costly for two reasons:

· The property may be subject to property tax re-appraisal.

· The $250,000 capital gains exemption on the portion of the property in the trust may be lost because the exemption applies to only the individual.

Instead, Mr. Abts recommends the use of the "ledger" method, as it only applies after the death of the first spouse. The ledger method will only allocate assets to the survivor's A sub-trust and the decedent's B sub-trust and/or C sub-trust. When a real estate deed is retitled, he recommends that a Trust Warranty Deed (as opposed to a Quit Claim Deed or a Grant Deed) be used because it allows you to retain the original warranties (unlike a Grant Deed which only passes title to the property). This is a complicated subject, and we recommend consulting Mr. Abts' book for more detail. Be sure to keep copies of all real estate deeds with your other living trust documents. Keep the originals in a safe deposit box.

Business Interests

If the decedent owned a business or was a partner in one and placed his or her interest in the living trust, you will need to consider getting a valuation at the time of death and six months later. Hopefully, the decedent had the foresight to include any and all business agreements with living trust documents. If not, look for the IRS Schedule C form. It identifies any deductions related to businesses. Also look for a Buy/Sell agreement. As described below, business interests can take a variety of forms.

- **Sole Proprietorship**. This is a common form of business ownership. Proprietorships are owned and operated by one person or a married couple. Sole proprietorships can be placed into a living trust via a Bill of Sale or Letter of Transfer. Sole proprietorships are at risk of decline or failure after the death of the owner. Therefore, if the business is to be sold, it should be done quickly after the person's death and while the business is still operating in an optimal fashion.

- **Partnership**. As the name suggests, partnerships consist of two or more partners who join together to own and operate a business. In terms of settling trust assets, it is helpful if there is a formal partnership agreement. However, this is not always the case. If there is no formal agreement, then a Bill of Sale/ Letter of Transfer can be used to place the partnership into a living trust. Depending on the situation, the surviving partner can continue the business by him- or herself and take sole responsibility for any new liabilities. If it is advantageous to continue the partnership, then a new agreement should be drawn up to protect the interests of all parties.

- **Family Limited Partnership (FLP)**. This is a good method of reducing or eliminating estate taxes and guarding against potential lawsuits. It is a method of holding property that combines advantages of holding property as a corporation with the advantages of owning property in a partnership. All FLPs have one thing in common: They are all run by the general partners only. No limited partner has a vote or voice in the administration and management of the partnership business. You may have a situation in which the general partner may only own 1 or 2 percent of the assets but will control all those assets.

  It is common in an FLP for the parents to place their assets into the partnership. In the beginning they are both the general partners and the limited partners. Later, depending on the form of FLP, they gift their limited partnership interests to their children. The effect of an FLP is that the parents essentially have given up ownership of the assets but retain control. The FLP is dissolved upon the death of the general partner, but that partnership can be reinstated by the surviving partners. The reinstatement must be done quickly after the date of death (within two months). If the decedent's B or C trust is to include any part of an FLP, the surviving trustee must be a partner in the family limited partnership. The assets must be appraised and documented both on the creation of the FLP and after the death of the partner.

Limited Partnership. A limited partnership consists of one or more general partners and one or more limited partners. The general partners may run the operations of the business, and the limited partners may provide capital and help arrange financing without taking an active role in running the business. In return for their investment, they receive a share of the profits for their involvement as limited partners. A key feature of a limited partnership agreement lies in the area of liability, which falls on the general partners and not on the limited partners.

If the estate contained an investment in a limited partnership, you can get a valuation by writing to the general partner and requesting the information of the decedent's share of the partnership as of the date of death. As with a family limited partnership, the limited partnership dissolves upon the death of the general partner. The partners may quickly (within two months) reinstate the partnership with the agreement of all remaining partners. If a limited partner dies, the partnership can continue since limited partners are not actively involved in the operation of the business. If the limited partnership is placed in the decedent's B and/or C trust, the surviving trustee must be named as a limited partner.

- **Limited Liability Companies (LLCs)**. This is a relatively new and hybrid form of ownership that combines the properties of a corporation and partnership. LLCs are a "pass through" tax entity where company profits and losses are passed through the business and only taxed on the members' individual tax returns.

  In terms of estates and living trusts, a limited liability corporation has one big advantage — asset protection. For example, a person could launch a lawsuit against the LLC in the form of a "charging order," which means if they win they have the right to part or all of the income of the corporation. Even if the person wins, he or she does not get an interest in the corporation. More important, the LLC is not required to make any cash distributions, thus the creditor ends up with nothing. Worse, the creditor may have income tax liability and no money to pay for it. An LLC is a powerful deterrent against lawsuits.

- **Corporations**. A corporation is a legal entity owned by one or more shareholders (in the form of stock certificates). They can be public or private. In this instance, we are referring to a "C" corporation. In the case of a living trust, the stock certificates need to be retitled in the name of the individual's living trust. One of the advantages of a corporation is that it continues to live on after the death of a sole owner, and there is little regulatory red tape to contend with. The corporate income is chargeable to the corporation for purposes of income tax. If the income passes through to the shareholders, that income is considered a dividend and taxed again to the individual shareholder as ordinary income. Thus, the disadvantage of a "C" corporation is that it is taxed twice — once when the business makes a profit and then when those profits are distributed to shareholders. This disadvantage is avoided in the case of an "S" corporation.

• **S Corporation**. A major advantage of the S (or Sub S) corporation is that it avoids double taxation by passing all tax liabilities on to shareholders. As such, S corporations are only taxed once. In terms of a living trust, if the spouse dies holding an interest in such a corporation and leaves his or her stock to the surviving spouse, the trust can continue to hold the stock — if the trustee powers have a provision for such a situation. Moreover, if the surviving spouse is the sole income recipient, the decedent's share of the S corporation stock can be placed in the decedent's B trust. In addition, if it qualifies, the decedent's share can be placed into a QTIP or QDOT trust. In this case, it is required that the surviving spouse must have the right to all income from the B and C trusts.

Also, the trust language must permit the holding of the S corporation stock, but only in the event if the surviving spouse is the sole income beneficiary of the QTIP or QDOT trust. Because the survivor's A trust is revocable as long as the survivor lives, the surviving spouse may hold the survivor's share in his or her A trust.

If the trust is authorized to do so and if the beneficiaries are all named as having a beneficial interest in the stock shares, the trust can continue to hold the S stock upon the death of the surviving spouse (or individual, if single). To maintain the S election after the trustor's death, the beneficiaries must consent to the S election (IRS Form 2553, Election by a Small Business Corporation). Upon the death of the surviving spouse (or individual, if single) and the election to keep the S corporation within the living trust, the corporation must then issue a separate form (Form 1120 with Schedule K-1) to each beneficiary of the trust. After an S corporation status is elected, all corporate income is then distributed to the beneficiaries, and it is taxable to them on the Form 1040 Individual Income Tax Return. In the case of a surviving spouse, the income/loss that comes from the S corporation to the decedent's B trust and/ or C trust flows to the surviving spouse. Therefore, it must be reported on Form 1040 as well.

All beneficiaries must know that this is taxable income apart from the corporation's cash flow. There is bureaucratic red tape involved upon the death of an individual. To avoid this, a limited liability corporation may be a better vehicle than an S corporation.

· **Professional Corporation**. This is a corporation with purposes limited to professional services such as the services provided by doctors, dentists, attorneys, and other professionals. A professional corporation is formed under laws that specify exactly which professionals can incorporate in this entity. According to the tax code, only a professional can participate in a professional corporation unless the surviving spouse is also a professional. Such a corporation must be sold or ended within two months following the death of the professional.

If a group of professionals was involved in incorporation, they should have a Buy/Sell Agreement in place to cover the deaths of members and fund the agreement with life insurance policies. This establishes the value of the decedent's corporate interest. Funds from the life insurance proceeds can then pay for the decedent's interest in the professional corporation.

Neither a trust nor a non-professional is able to hold an interest in a professional corporation. If the professional corporation is a single enterprise (for example, a doctor or dentist), then that corporation must be liquidated. In this case, the assets may be money due (receivables) and equipment. It is in your interest to sell the assets quickly, as depreciation of them can occur rapidly.

Bankruptcy

A trust cannot file for bankruptcy. However, if the assets in a trust are not sufficient, there is a priority for paying creditors:

1. Employee income

2. Employee withholding taxes, federal and state taxes

3. Creditors.

If there are insufficient assets, the trustees should consider allocating the remaining assets on a percentage basis. The recommended allocation should be submitted to a probate court for approval. If the court grants its approval, the trustees bear no more responsibility.

Personal Effects

Personal effects are any asset that does not have a specific title, such as antiques, artwork, china, clothing, furniture, fixtures, furs, jewelry, and personal mementos. A common mistake is to over-value these items. While they mean much to the owners, they may not be of the same value to others because they reflect the owners' individual tastes. Over-valuation can result in higher taxes and end up in a loss rather than a gain for beneficiaries.

Guideline 6: Get the Details Right

Any settlement means dealing with the IRS and following its rules. This is not necessarily difficult, but omission of a step can be costly; it pays to understand and follow them. Follow these steps to satisfy IRS and tax court expectations.

Step 1: Create a separate bank account.

This step will keep the IRS happy and prevent you from losing the decedent's federal income tax deduction. Here is why this step is so important: Upon the death of the first spouse, the decedent's B and/or C trust becomes irrevocable. If you were the surviving spouse and used the assets of the decedent's B and/or C trust as your own, then the IRS will deem them as your (the survivor's) assets. That means the assets in these trusts lose their right of exemption against taxes — you will have forfeited the decedent's federal estate tax exemption. (The exemption rises to $3.5 million by 2009, so the tax burden could be substantial.) When the first spouse dies, create a separate bank account for the decedent's B and/or C trust (the same account can be used for both). This account should only be used for transactions directly related to the decedent's situation.

Step 2: Obtain and complete Form 56.

This form is the "Notice of Fiduciary Relationship" and can be downloaded from the IRS Web site. Its purpose is to give notice to the IRS of the deceased's death and to identify your fiduciary relationship as "Personal Representative of the Estate." It also identifies the name of the trust. Complete the form and send a copy of the trust document along with it when submitted. According to the IRS Web site:

> The term fiduciary means any person acting for another person. It applies to persons who have

positions of trust on behalf of others. A personal representative for a decedent's estate is a fiduciary. If you are appointed to act in any fiduciary capacity for another, you must file a written notice with the IRS stating this. Form 56, Notice Concerning Fiduciary Relationship, can be used for this purpose. The instructions and other requirements are given on the back of the form. You should file the written notice (or Form 56) as soon as the necessary information (including the EIN) is available. It notifies the IRS that, as the fiduciary, you are assuming the powers, rights, duties, and privileges of the decedent, and allows the IRS to mail to you all tax notices concerning the person (or estate) you represent. The notice remains in effect until you notify the appropriate IRS office that your relationship to the estate has terminated.

This language seems to indicate that filing a Form 56 is required. However, Henry W. Abts III recommends against use of this form. He finds the step unnecessary and feels that other steps (described below) accomplish the same purpose without letting the IRS see the details of the trust. Check the latest IRS regulations regarding this form or have an attorney do it for you.

Step 3: Obtain and complete Form SS-4.

This form needs to be filled out and sent to the IRS to obtain an Employer Identification Number (EIN). Although you are not an employer, the EIN is valid for living trusts. This form can be downloaded from the IRS Web site. The EIN is used for the B and C trusts when the first spouse dies. It is also used for the

A, B, and/or C trusts upon the death of the second spouse and for the A trust when a single person dies.

Step 4: Allocate the assets.

There are different methods of asset allocation. Perhaps the clearest and simplest (for both you and the IRS) is the trust ledger method showing the assets. It serves as a record of:

- All trust money received (including money to be invested on behalf of the beneficiary)

- All account disbursements

- The balance held in trust

The trust ledger also shows other valuable property received on behalf of a beneficiary. When trust assets change or are altered, such as by transferring assets into or out of a given trust or between trusts, the law may require the administrator to do three things:

- Update the changes in the ledger as transfers in assets occur.

- Generate and store separate asset transfer documents.

- Record or file asset transfer documentation with governmental entities.

Use the ledger method to allocate assets to the decedent's B and/ or C trust and then transfer them to the appropriate subtrust.

This method applies only after the death of the first spouse and only in allocation of assets to the decedent's B and/or C trust and to the survivor's A trust. The method does not need to be used when the second spouse dies (or a single person dies).

Different states use different methods for asset allocations. For example, in separate property states, the survivor's share of the assets does not receive stepped-up valuation, and the ledger worksheet will be different from a community property state. When completing any ledger, use the net value of the assets (the current market value of the estate) minus any outstanding liabilities (mortgages and other debts).

Step 5: Decide which assets will be distributed or retained

After allocation of assets into the separate trusts, you need to decide to identify three categories of assets:

- Those to be retained in the trust for the surviving spouse

- Those to be distributed directly to the heirs or beneficiaries

- Those to be distributed later to heirs or beneficiaries

In these three areas, you also have to decide which assets should be sold as-is and which should be sold and converted into income (for example, stocks or mutual funds). If the circumstances of the surviving spouse warrant it, you may also want to consider converting specific growth assets into income-producing assets to provide for payment of necessary living expenses.

Step 6: Distribute personal effects

Next, distribute personal effects as specified in the Trust Memorandum, a document that holds legal authority. The memorandum should list all important personal effects and where they should be distributed. In the event there is no memorandum, then distribution will have to be worked out among the heirs and/or beneficiaries. Jealousy and hurt feelings can arise among family members in this situation, particularly in the case of second marriages. It is so important to include a Memorandum of Trust in the initial setup of a living trust. It does not have to be a complicated document, as shown in the example below.

SAMPLE: MEMORANDUM OF TRUST			
For Distribution of Personal Property			
Upon my death, it is my wish that the following personal property items be distributed to specific individuals as indicated below:			
Personal Property Items	Recipient	Date	Initial
Sears Craftsman table saw of Dan Smith	Joe Smith (son)	02/02/2007	
Spode "Blue Italian" bone china — 5-piece place setting of Eileen Smith	Sue Smith (daughter)	02/02/2007	

Although it is not absolutely necessary, it can be helpful to be as specific as possible (as shown above) when listing items. This can be helpful in instances where there are multiple items in the same category. For example, there may be more than one set of china from different manufacturers. If these sets are not specified, then it can be unclear as to which set is to be distributed to whom.

Step 7: Maintain a record of expenses for the last illness and the funeral

Last illness and funeral expenses can be deducted on the deceased person's 1040 individual income tax return or on the 706 federal estate tax return (if required). The 1040 form must be filed upon the death of the surviving spouse or a single person by the trustee or executor.

Step 8: Complete and file Form 1040

To benefit from potential tax advantages, the surviving spouse should file a joint Form 1040 Individual Tax Income form for the year in which his or her spouse died. Single returns do not offer the tax advantages offered by joint returns, so it makes sense to take this step. The same individual social security number is used to report all income. In preparing the form, review the decedent's income tax forms for the past three to five years because there may be deductions that can be included to reduce the tax burden.

Step 9: Complete and file Form 1041

This is the U.S. Income Tax Return for Estates and Trust form. It is an income tax information form for the decedent's B and/or C trust. A Form 1041 is filed for the decedent's asset shares that are retained in trust. Its purpose is to identify the income generated from within the irrevocable trust. It should also be filed for the remainder of the months of the year of the decedent's death because assets may be kept in trust for the surviving spouse. As long as income is generated from within the trust, Form 1041 should be filed on a yearly basis. Form 1041 (accompanied by Schedule K-1 forms) may be simply an information form because the trust income normally goes to the surviving spouse (or the beneficiaries when there is no surviving spouse). Thus the form simply shows that all income from the trust was paid out and there is no trust income tax to pay. Any income retained inside a trust is currently taxed at nearly 39.6 percent.

It is a good idea to file a Form 1041 form for the first year after the death of the decedent to establish that you have an irrevocable trust. If the trust generates less than $700 of annual income, however, it is not necessary to file the 1041 form. An irrevocable trust does not have the right to carry forward a loss. Instead, you should place any asset with a loss in the survivor's trust (or heirs' trust). This will provide them with a tax loss "carry forward" on their individual income tax returns.

Step 10: Complete Schedule K-1

This form accompanies the Form 1041 tax return. It identifies who is the recipient of the irrevocable trust's income. If the surviving spouse (or an individual) has died, then the trust income normally passes to the heirs. Schedule K-1 forms are required to include the surviving spouse's and/or the heirs' social security numbers.

Step 11: Complete Form 706 (if necessary)

Form 706 is the United States Estate (and Generation-Skipping Transfer) Tax Return. This is filed only when estate taxes are due or a QTIP election needs to be made. At this writing, this form does not need to be filed when the value of an estate is less than $2 million. If the value of the trust goes over the exemption levels, then you must complete and file Form 706 — all 40 pages of it (including instructions and schedules). You may need an accountant to complete this horrendous form. Be sure to select one who has considerable experience and expertise in this area. The taxes will need to be paid within nine months.

Step 12: Determine if inheritance taxes are due

The matter of inheritance taxes will depend on which state you live in. How a state inheritance tax is levied depends on the state. You may need to deal with one of the following alternatives:

- The inheritance tax may not imposed upon the first spouse's death, only after the death of the surviving spouse.

- An inheritance tax may be imposed on the estate after the death of the first spouse.

- A separate additional tax may be imposed on the estate of a single person.

You will need to check with the appropriate tax department in your state to get the current requirements as regulations can change. As inheritance tax issues can be complex, you may want to engage the services of an attorney experienced in this area. If an inheritance tax is due, you will have to file an inventory of the assets and an affidavit that certifies the inventory is true.

Step 13: Complete a certification of the trust

Financial and other institutions may require a Certification of Trust from the successor trustee before they allow access to the assets of the trust. This simple form can be created and included with other trust documents. As the trust is amended, these amendments can be included in the certification document. A Certification of Trust can prevent delays caused by cautious financial institutions and others who are either hidebound by their rules or are not familiar with estate settlements.

Step 14: Spell out responsibilities in writing

This step is obviously not truly the last one. It should be considered in light of all the previous steps. It is an important task, however, since it makes clear to everyone involved what their responsibilities are and when they should be carried out. The step can include such items as checking the safe deposit box, paying debts, closing credit card accounts, and filing appropriate tax forms. If this task is not completed, things can fall through the cracks and end up being expensive.

Dependency Indemnity Compensation (DIC)

Dependency Indemnity Compensation is a monthly benefit

paid to eligible survivors of:

- a military service member who died while on active duty OR

- a veteran whose death resulted from a service-related injury or disease OR

- a veteran whose death resulted from a non service-related injury or disease, and who was receiving, or was entitled to receive, VA Compensation for service-connected disability that was rated as totally disabling

  - for at least 10 years immediately before death OR

  - since the veteran's release from active duty and for at least five years immediately preceding death, OR

  - for at least one year before death if the veteran was a former prisoner of war who died after September 30, 1999.

Who Is Eligible?

The surviving spouse is eligible for DIC if he or she:

- validly married the veteran before January 1, 1957, OR

- was married to a service member who died on active duty, OR

- married the veteran within 15 years of discharge from the period of military service in which the disease or injury that caused the veteran's death began or was aggravated, OR

- was married to the veteran for at least one year, OR

- had a child with the veteran, AND

- cohabited with the veteran continuously until the veteran's death or, if separated, was not at fault for the separation, AND

- is not currently remarried. A surviving spouse who remarries on or after December 16, 2003, and on or after attaining age 57, is entitled to continue to receive DIC.

The surviving child or children are eligible to receive DIC benefits if he or she is:

- not included on the surviving spouse's DIC

- unmarried AND

- under age 18, or between the ages of 18 and 23 and attending school.

Certain helpless adult children are also entitled to DIC.

A surviving parent may also be eligible for an income-based benefit.

How Much Does VA Pay?

The current basic monthly rate of DIC is $1,067 for an eligible surviving spouse. The rate is increased for each dependent child and also if the surviving spouse is housebound or needs aid and attendance. The Veteran's Administraton also adds a transitional benefit of $250 to the surviving spouse's monthly DIC if there are children under age 18. The amount is based on a family unit, not individual children. Benefit rate tables, including those for children alone and parents, are published on the Internet at **www.vba.va.gov/bln/21/Rates**.

How Should a Claimant Apply?

Claimants should complete VA Form 21-534 Application for Dependency and Indemnity Compensation, Death Pension, and Accrued Benefits by a Surviving Spouse or Child.

16
Are There Living Trust Scams?

Yes, there are scams. Criminals love to target senior citizens because they may be more vulnerable to the confusing and false pitches.

To avoid becoming a victim, be aware of the common tactics of scam artists. Living trust "mills" advertise on the Internet, through the mail, by sponsoring seminars, or even by using the old-fashioned technique of going door-to-door. They will try to assume a mantle of respectability and trust by using names that sound like true non-profit organizations. The American Association of Retired People (AARP) is a prime example. Companies will try to use names close to AARP to convince you that they are endorsed by this organization when they are not.

The Alliance for Mature Americans, for example, stole millions of dollars from an estimated 10,000 seniors in California. These scam artists used questionnaires to find out every detail of unsuspecting peoples' finances, then convinced their victims that their savings were not safe unless they were in a living trust (or annuities, or whatever other fraudulent instrument the company was promoting). The company's representatives then earned money off commissions (plus other income) while their victims lost their money. California's Attorney General successfully closed down the company and won a $200 million dollar judgment against it.

Beware of exaggerated claims regarding living trusts. Scam artists will inflate the costs and complications of probate. Probate can be costly, but those costs vary by state — it pays to know your state laws. The criminals may claim that living trusts will reduce your income taxes, which is not true.

Another claim scam artists make is that living trusts are cheaper than wills, which is also not true. They may also claim that if you have a living trust you do not need a will. You need a pour-over will to account for all property not listed in your living trust. They may even try to convince you that the salesperson is an attorney and is an expert on living trusts. Finally, a scam artist may claim that creditors cannot go after your property if it is in a living trust, but a living trust does not offer protection from creditors.

Appendix
Sample Forms

REVOCABLE LIVING TRUST FOR AN INDIVIDUAL

Article I: Declarations

This Revocable Living Trust Agreement is made this _____ _____ (day, month, year) between _____ (name) of _____(address, city, state) herein referred to as Grantor_____ (name) of _____(address, city, state) herein referred to as co-trustees.

Whereas, I am now, as Grantor, the owner of the property described in the attached Schedule A and

Whereas, I desire to make provision for the care and management of said property, and the collection of the income from that property, and the disposition of both said income and such property in the manner herein provided:

Now, therefore, for the reasons set forth above, and in consideration of the mutual agreements set forth herein, I, as Grantor, and the Trustees agree as to the following:

ARTICLE II: TRUST PROPERTY DISPOSITION DURING MY LIFETIME

1. Property Transfer: I, as Grantor, in consideration of the acceptance

REVOCABLE LIVING TRUST FOR AN INDIVIDUAL

by trustee of the trust herein created, hereby transfer, assign, and deliver to Trustees, their Successors in trust and Assigns, the property described in attached Schedule A.

2. Disposition of Income and Principal: The Trustee(s) shall manage the trust estate and collect the income derived from the trust assets. After the payment of all taxes and assessments and all charges incident to the management thereof, the Trustee(s) shall dispose of the net income therefrom as follows:

During my lifetime, the Trustees may pay income of the trust estate and such portions of the principal as the Grantor from time to time may direct, to the Grantor, or otherwise as I direct during my life. After my death, the Successor Trustee shall distribute the trust estate to the following beneficiary) who survive me:

Beneficiary 1: (names and addresses)

_____

_____

_____

Beneficiary 2:

_____

_____

_____

ARTICLE III: DISTRIBUTIONS TO BENEFICIARIES UNDER LEGAL AGE

1. For any beneficiary under the age of 21 years, his/her share shall not be paid to said beneficiary but shall instead be held in trust to apply to his/her use of all the income thereof, and also such amounts of the principal, even to the extent of all, as the trustee considers necessary or suitable for the support, welfare, and education of said beneficiary(ies). When he/she attains the age of 21 years, the Trustee shall pay him/her the remaining principal, if any.

REVOCABLE LIVING TRUST FOR AN INDIVIDUAL

2. If any trust beneficiary should die before having received all the principal thereof, then the remaining principal shall be paid to his/her then living child or children (equally if more than one), and in default thereof, to the then living descendants of the grantor, per stirpes*.

3. No trust interest shall be transferable or assignable by any beneficiary, or be subject during his or her life to the claims of his or her creditors.

4. The trusts hereunder shall terminate not later than twenty-one (21) years after the death of the last beneficiary name herein.

*This is a Latin term. It designates a system of inheritance under which children take among them the share which their parent would have taken had he or she survived the decedent. Thus, the children are said to claim their shares by representing their parent.

ARTICLE IV: RIGHT OF REVOCATION AND AMENDMENT

1. Revocation and Amendment: By signed instrument delivered to the trustee, the Grantor retains the right to revoke the trusts hereunder, in whole or in part, or amend this Agreement from time to time in any manner so desired.

ARTICLE V: DESIGNATION OF SUCCESSOR TRUSTEES

1. Successor Trustees: In the event of the death or incapacity of both trustees, I hereby nominate and appoint as Successor Trustee_____(name) of _____

_____

(address, city, state). In the event the successor trustee declines to serve or is unable to serve, I appoint the first designated beneficiary hereunder. The trustees and their successors shall serve without bond.

Trustees' Acceptance: This trust has been accepted by trustees and will be administered in the State of _____

REVOCABLE LIVING TRUST FOR AN INDIVIDUAL

(name) and its validity, construction, and all rights thereunder shall be governed by the laws of that state.

In Witness Whereof, Grantors and Trustees have executed this Agreement on the date above written.

_____   _____

Grantor   Co-Trustee

_____   _____

Witness 1   Co-Trustee

_____   _____

Witness 1   Witness 2

Sworn to and subscribed before me this _____(day) of _____(month and year).

My commission expires: _____

                              Notary Public

_____ Date

Schedule A

The following is a list of property and assets included in this trust agreement:

_____

_____

_____

_____

_____

_____

_____

SAMPLE AB LIVING TRUST

Between:_____ (your names) as Trustees._____ (your names), residents of the state of _____ (state name) establish a Trust upon the purpose and conditions set forth hereafter.

Declaration of Trust

Article I. Trust Name

This trust shall be known as The_____ (name) Living Trust.

Article II. Trust Property

A. Property Placed in Trust _____ _____, called the grantors or trustees, declare that they have set aside and hold in The _____ (name) Living Trust all their interest in the property described in the attached Schedules (A, B, C, etc.). The trust property shall be used for the benefit of the trust beneficiaries and shall be administered and distributed by the trustees in accordance with this Declaration of Trust.

B. Rights Retained by Grantors

As long as both grantors are alive, both grantors retain all rights to all income, profits, and control of the trust property listed on Schedule A of The ____ _____ (name) Living Trust.

1. As long as _____ (wife's name) is alive, she shall retain all rights to all income, profits, and control of her separate property listed on Schedule B of The _____ (name) Living Trust.

2. As long as _____ (husband's name) is alive, he shall retain all rights to all income, profits, and control of his separate property listed on Schedule C of The _____ (name) Living Trust.

SAMPLE AB LIVING TRUST

C. Additional or After-Acquired Property

Either grantor, or both, may add property to the trust at any time.

D. Character of Property Placed in Trust

While both grantors are alive, property transferred to this trust shall retain its original character. If the trust is revoked, the trustee shall distribute the trust property to the grantors based on the same ownership rights they had before the property was transferred to the trust. Specifically:

1. Shared Property

   All trust property listed on Schedule A is shared property: (Describe property in Schedule A).

2. Separate Property

   The trust property listed on Schedule B shall retain its character as the separate property of _____ _____ (wife's name). The trust property listed on Schedule C shall retain its character as the separate property of _____ _____(husband's name).

   (Note: If either party has no separate property, indicate so.)

E. Revocation and Amendment

The _____ (name) Living Trust may be revoked att any time by writing given to the other grantor. No beneficiary need be given any notice of revocation. The Trust may be amended at any time with the signature of both Grantors. After the death of a spouse, the surviving spouse can amend his or her revocable living trust, Trust B,

F. Residence Rights

Grantors have the right to possess and occupy their principal

SAMPLE AB LIVING TRUST

residence for life, rent-free and without charge, except for taxes, insurance, maintenance, and any related costs and expenses.

Article III. Trustees

A. Original Trustees

The trustees of The _____ (name) Living Trust created under this Declaration of Trust shall be _____ (your names). Either trustee may act for, and represent, the trust, in any transaction.

B. Trustee on Death or Incapacity of Original Trustee

Upon the death or incapacity, of _____ (wife's name) or _____ (husband's name), the other spouse shall serve as sole trustee of this trust and all trusts and any child's trusts created under this Declaration of Trust.

C. Trustee's Responsibility

The trustee in office shall serve as trustee of this trust and all trusts and any child's trust created under this Declaration of Trust.

D. Terminology

In this Declaration of Trust, the term "trustee" includes any successor trustee or trustees.

E. Successor Trustee

Upon the death or incapacity of the surviving spouse, or the incapacity of both spouses, the successor trustee shall be _____ _____ (name/ names). If any one or all are unable to serve or to continue serving as successor trustee, the next successor trustee shall be _____ (name).

SAMPLE AB LIVING TRUST

F. Trustee Resignation

Any trustee in office may resign at any time by signing a notice of resignation. The written resignation must be delivered to the person or institution that is either named in this Declaration of Trust, or appointed by the trustee to serve as the trustee.

G. Power to Appoint Successor Trustee

If all the named successor trustees cease to, or are unable to, serve as trustee, any trustee may appoint an additional successor trustee or trustees to serve in the order nominated. The appointment must be made in writing, signed by the trustee, and notarized accordingly.

H. Waiver of Bond

No bond shall be required of any trustee.

I. Compensation

No trustee shall receive any compensation for serving as trustee, except that he or she shall be entitled to reasonable compensation, as determined by the trustee.

J. Trustee Liability

With respect to the exercise or non-exercise of discretionary powers granted by this trust, the trustee shall not be liable for actions taken in good faith.

Article IV. Specific Beneficiaries

A. Wife's Specific and Alternate Beneficiaries

Upon the death of _____ (wife's name), the following gifts shall be made from trust property owned by _____ (wife's name).

   1. _____ (beneficiary name/ names) shall be given_____

SAMPLE AB LIVING TRUST

(identification of property). If _____
(beneficiary) does not survive _____
(wife's name), that property shall be given to _____
_____ (alternate beneficiary).

2. _____ (beneficiary name/
names) shall be given_____
___ (identification of property). If _____
(beneficiary) does not survive _____
(wife's name), that property shall be given to _____
_____(alternate beneficiary).

3. _____ (beneficiary name/
names) shall be given_____
___ (identification of property). If _____
(beneficiary) does not survive _____
(wife's name), that property shall be given to _____
_____(alternate beneficiary).

B. Husband's Specific and Alternate Beneficiaries

Upon the death of _____
(husband's name) the following gifts shall be made from trust
property owned by _____
(husband's name).

1. _____ (beneficiary
name/names) shall be given _____
_____ (identification of property). If
_____ does not survive
_____ (husband's name), that
property shall be given to _____
(alternate beneficiary).

2. _____
_____ (beneficiary name/names) shall be given
_____ (identification of property).
If _____ does not survive

SAMPLE AB LIVING TRUST

_____ (husband's name), that property shall be given to _____ (alternate beneficiary).

3. _____
_____ (beneficiary name/names) shall be given _____ (identification of property). If _____ does not survive _____ (husband's name), that property shall be given to _____ (alternate beneficiary).

C. Remaining Trust Property

Except as provided otherwise in this trust document, all other trust property of the deceased spouse shall be transferred to, and administered as part of Trust A.

Article V. Creation of Trust A Upon First Death

A. Terminology

1. The first grantor to die shall be called the "deceased spouse." The living grantor shall then be called the "surviving spouse."

2. The "trust property of the deceased spouse" shall consist of all property of The _____ (name) Living Trust individually owned by the deceased spouse at the time it was transferred to the trustee. In addition, all property shall include:

_____

_____

_____

(Itemize other property: e.g., shared ownership property, accumulated income, value appreciation of the ownership interest of the deceased spouse, etc.)

SAMPLE AB LIVING TRUST

3. The "trust property of the surviving spouse" shall consist of all property of The _____ (name) Living Trust individually owned by the surviving spouse at the time it was transferred to the trustee. In addition, all property shall include:

    (Itemize other property: e.g., shared ownership property, accumulated income, value appreciation of the ownership interest of the surviving spouse, etc.)

B. Division of Trust Property on Death of Deceased Spouse

1. Upon the death of the deceased spouse, the trustee shall divide the property of The _____ (your names) Living Trust listed on Schedules A, B, and C into two separate trusts, Trust A and Trust B.

2. All trust assets of the deceased spouse shall be placed in a trust known as Trust A, the Marital Life Estate Trust, after making any specific gifts subject to any provision in this Declaration of Trust that creates child's trusts or creates custodianship under the Uniform Transfers to Minors Act.

3. The trustee shall place all trust assets of the surviving spouse in a trust known as Trust B (The Surviving Spouse's Trust).

4. Physical segregation of the assets of The _____ (your name) Living Trust is not required to divide that trust's property into Trust A and Trust B. The trustee shall exclusively determine what records, documents, and actions are required to establish and maintain Trust A and Trust B.

C. Trust A Administration

All property held in Trust A shall be administered as follows:

1. Upon the death of the deceased spouse, Trust A shall be irrevocable.

SAMPLE AB LIVING TRUST

2. The life beneficiary of Trust A shall be the surviving spouse.

3. If _____ (wife's name) is the deceased spouse, the final beneficiaries of Trust A shall be: _____.

   If _____ (wife's name) is the deceased spouse, the alternate final beneficiaries of Trust A shall be: _____.

4. If _____ (husband's name) is the deceased spouse, the final beneficiaries of Trust A shall be: _ _____.

   If _____ (husband's name) is the deceased spouse, the alternate final beneficiaries of Trust A shall be: _____.

5. The trustee shall pay to or spend for the benefit of the surviving spouse the net income of Trust A at least quarterly. The trustee shall also pay to or spend for the benefit of the surviving spouse any sums from the principal of Trust A necessary for the surviving spouse's health, education, support, and maintenance, in accord with his or her accustomed manner of living.

6. No accounting of Trust A shall be required of the trustee, except that the final beneficiaries shall be provided with copies of the annual federal income tax return.

7. The trustee shall be entitled to reasonable compensation from assets of Trust A for services rendered managing Trust A, without court approval.

8. Upon the death of the life beneficiary, the trustee shall distribute the property of Trust A to the final beneficiary or beneficiaries.

SAMPLE AB LIVING TRUST

Article VI. Trust B: The Surviving Spouse's Trust

A. Creation of Trust B, The Surviving Spouse's Trust

Upon the death of the deceased spouse, all trust property owned by the surviving spouse shall be held in Trust B, The Surviving Spouse's Trust.

B. Trust B Administration

Until the death of the surviving spouse, the surviving spouse retains all rights to all income, profits, and control of the property in Trust B. The surviving spouse may amend or revoke Trust B at any time during his or her lifetime, without notifying any beneficiary.

C. Distribution of Property in Trust B

1. Upon the death of the surviving spouse, Trust B becomes irrevocable.

2. The trustee shall first distribute any specific gifts of the surviving spouse to the named beneficiaries. The trustee shall then distribute all remaining property of Trust B to his or her final, or alternate final, named beneficiaries.

3. All distributions are subject to any provision in this Declaration of Trust that creates child's trusts or creates custodianships under the Uniform Transfers to Minors Act.

Article VII. Incapacity

A. Grantors Incapacity

If both grantors become physically or mentally incapacitated and are no longer able to manage this trust, the person or persons named as successor trustee shall serve as trustee. Those persons listed below shall determine the grantors' capacity when the successor trustee(s) request their opinions. For incapacity to be decided, the majority of these persons must state, in writing

SAMPLE AB LIVING TRUST

decided, the majority of these persons must state, in writing, that in their opinion the grantors are no longer reasonably capable of serving as trustee. In that event, the successor trustee shall serve as trustee.

_____

_____

_____

On a minimum annual basis, the successor trustee shall pay trust income to, or for the benefit of, the grantors. The successor trustee may also spend any amount of trust principal necessary, in his or her discretion, for the needs of the grantors until a licensed physician certifies that the grantors, or either of them, are no longer incapacitated or until their deaths.

B. Amending AB Trust If Estate Tax Law Changes

Not withstanding any other provision of this trust, if Congress changes the estate tax law, this trust may be amended as follows:

1. If both grantors are alive but one is incapacitated, the competent spouse may amend this AB Trust in order to take best advantage of the new tax law.

2. If both grantors are alive but incapacitated, the successor trustee may amend this AB Trust in order to take best advantage of the new tax law.

C. Incapacity of Surviving Spouse

If, after the death of the deceased spouse, the surviving spouse becomes physically or mentally incapacitated and is no longer able to manage Trust B, the person or persons named as successor trustee shall serve as trustee.

1. The determination of the grantor's capacity to manage the trust shall be made by those of the persons listed below who are

SAMPLE AB LIVING TRUST

reasonably available when the successor trustee (or any of them, if two or more are named to serve together) requests their opinion. If a majority of these persons state, in writing, that in their opinion the grantor is no longer reasonably capable of serving as trustee, the successor trustee shall serve as trustee.

_____

_____

_____

2. On a minimum annual basis, the successor trustee shall pay trust income at least annually to, or for the benefit of, the surviving spouse, and spend any amount of that trust's principal necessary in the successor trustee's discretion, for the needs of the surviving spouse, until the surviving spouse is no longer incapacitated, or until his or her death. Any income in excess of amounts spent for the benefit of the surviving spouse shall be accumulated and added to the property of Trust B.

3. The successor trustee shall manage Trust A, under the terms of this Declaration of Trust, until the surviving spouse is again able to serve as trustee of that trust, or until the death of the surviving spouse.

4. The successor trustee shall manage any operational child's trust created by their Declaration of Trust.

Article VIII. Simultaneous Death

If both grantors should die simultaneously, or under such circumstances as to render it difficult or impossible to determine who predeceased the other, it shall be conclusively presumed that both died at the same moment, and neither shall be presumed to have survived the other for purposes of this living trust.

Article IX. Trustee's Powers and Duties

A. Powers Under State Law

SAMPLE AB LIVING TRUST

To carry out the provisions of this Declaration of Trust and to manage the trust property of The _____ (name Living Trust, Trust A, and Trust B, and any child's trust created under this Declaration of Trust, the trustee shall have all authority and power allowed or conferred under _____ (state name) law, subject to the trustee's fiduciary duty to the grantors and the beneficiaries.

B. Specified Powers

The trustee's powers include, but are not limited to:

1. The power to sell trust property, and to borrow money and to encumber property, specifically including:

   _____

   _____

   _____

(E.g., real estate, mortgage, deed of trust, etc.)

2. The power to manage trust real estate as if the trustee were the absolute owner of it, including the power to lease (even if the lease term may extend beyond the period of any trust) or grant options to lease the property, to make repairs or alterations, and to insure against loss.

3. The power to sell or grant options for the sale or exchange of any trust property. Such property includes:

   _____

   _____

   _____

   (E.g., stocks, bonds, debentures, and any other form of security or security account, etc.)

4. The power to invest trust property in property of any kind, including but not limited to:

SAMPLE AB LIVING TRUST

_____

_____

_____

(E.g, bonds, debentures, notes, mortgages, stocks, stock options, etc.)

5. The power to receive additional property from any source and add to any trust created by this Declaration of Trust.

6. The power to employ and pay reasonable fees to accountants, lawyers, or investment experts for information or advice relating to the trust.

7. The power to continue any business of either grantor.

8. The power to institute or defend legal actions concerning the trust or the grantors' affairs.

9. The power to execute any documents necessary to administer any trust created in this Declaration of Trust.

10. The power to diversify investments.

C. Payment by the Trustee of the Grantors' Debts and Taxes

1. Wife's Debts and Taxes

_____(wife's name) s debts and death taxes shall be paid by the trustee. The trustee shall pay these from the following trust property:

_____

_____

_____

2. Husband's Debts and Taxes_____

_____(husband's name) 's debts and death taxes shall be paid by the trustee. The trustee shall pay these from the following trust property:

SAMPLE AB LIVING TRUST

_____

_____

_____

3. If Specified Property Insufficient

If the property specified above is insufficient to pay all grantor's debts and death taxes, the trustee shall determine how such debts and death taxes shall be paid from that grantor's trust property, except as limited by any law, or IRS regulation, controlling the property in Trust A.

Article X. General Administrative Provisions

A. Controlling Law

The validity of The _____ (name) Living Trust and construction of its provisions shall be governed by the laws of _____ (state name).

B. Severability

If any trust provision is ruled unenforceable, the remaining provisions shall nevertheless remain in effect.

C. Amendments

The term "Declaration of Trust" includes any provisions added by valid amendment.

Article XI. Child's Trusts

All trust property left to any of the minor or young adult beneficiaries listed below shall be retained in trust for each such beneficiary in a separate trust of this _____ (name) Living Trust. Each trust may be identified and referred to by adding the name of that trust's beneficiary to the name of this trust. The following terms apply to each child's trust:

A. Trust Beneficiaries and Age Limits

SAMPLE AB LIVING TRUST

A child's trust shall end when the beneficiary of that trust, listed below, becomes 30, except as otherwise specified in this section:

Name(s) of Beneficiary   Age

_____

_____

_____

B. Powers and Duties of Child's Trust Trustee

1. Until a child's trust ends, the trustee may distribute to or use for the benefit of the beneficiary as much of the net income or principal of the child's trust as the trustee deems necessary for the beneficiary's health, support, maintenance, or education. Education includes, but is not limited to:

   _____

   _____

   _____

   (E.g., college, graduate, postgraduate, and vocational studies, and educated-related living expenses.)

2. Any child's trust income that is not distributed to a beneficiary by the trustee shall be accumulated and added to the principal of the trust for that beneficiary.

3. The trustee of a child's trust is not required to make any accounting or report to the trust beneficiary.

C. Assignment of Interest of Beneficiary Prohibited

The interests of the beneficiary of a child's trust shall not be transferable by voluntary or involuntary assignment or by operation of law before actual receipt by the beneficiary. These interests shall be free from the claims of creditors and from attachments, execution, bankruptcy, or other legal process to the fullest extent permitted by law.

SAMPLE AB LIVING TRUST

D. Trustee Compensation

Any trustee of a child's trust shall be entitled to reasonable compensation without court approval out of the trust assets for ordinary and extraordinary services, and for all services in connection with the termination of any trust.

E. Termination of Children's Trusts

A child's trust shall end when any of the following events occurs:

1. The beneficiary reaches the age of _____. If the trust ends for this reason, the remaining principal and accumulated income of the trust shall be given outright to the beneficiary.

2. The beneficiary dies. If the trust ends for this reason, the trust property shall pass to the beneficiary's heirs.

3. The trustee distributes all trust property under the provisions of this Declaration of Trust.

Article XII. Custodianships Under the Uniform Transfers to Minors Act

1. All property _____ (beneficiary) becomes entitled to under this trust document shall be given to _____ (custodian's name) as custodian for _____ (beneficiary) under the _____ (state name) Uniform Transfers to Minors Act, until _____ (beneficiary) reaches age _____.

2. All property _____ (beneficiary) becomes entitled to under this trust document shall be given to _____ (custodian's name) as custodian for _____ (beneficiary) under the _____ (state name) Uniform Transfers to Minors Act, until _____ (beneficiary) reaches age _____.

SAMPLE AB LIVING TRUST

3. All property _____ (beneficiary) becomes entitled to under this trust document shall be given to _____ (custodian's name) as custodian for _____ (beneficiary) under the _____ (state name) Uniform Transfers to Minors Act, until _____ (beneficiary) reaches age _____.

Certification by Grantors

We certify that we have read this Declaration of Trust and that it correctly states the terms and conditions under which the trust property is to be held, managed, and disposed of by the trustees, and we approve the Declaration of Trust.

Dated: _____

_____

Grantor and Trustee

Dated: _____

_____

Grantor and Trustee

Notary's Declaration and Acknowledgment

State of _____

County of _____

On _____, 20_____, before me, _____, a notary public in and for said state, personally appeared _____ _____, personally known to me (or proved to me on the basis of satisfactory evidence) to be the persons whose names are subscribed to the within Declaration of Trust, and acknowledged to me that they executed the same in their authorized capacities and

SAMPLE AB LIVING TRUST

that by their signatures on the instrument they executed the Declaration of Trust.

_____

Signature of Notary   Public

Schedule A

Shared Property Placed In Trust

_____
_____
_____
_____
_____

Schedule B

Wife's Separate Property Placed In Trust

_____
_____
_____
_____
_____

Schedule C

Husband's Separate Property Placed In Trust

_____
_____
_____
_____
_____

SAMPLE AB DISCLAIMER LIVING TRUST

Declaration Of Trust

Between: _____ (your names) as Trustees, residents of the state of _____ (state name), we establish a Trust pursuant to the purpose and conditions set forth hereafter.

Article I. Trust Name

This trust shall be known as The _____ (your names or name of trust if different) Living Trust.

Article II. Trust Property

A. Property Placed in Trust

_____ (your names), called the grantors or trustees, declare that we have set aside and hold in The _____ Living Trust all our interest in the property described in the attached Schedules A, B, and C.

B. Grantors' Retained Rights

As long as we (the grantors) are alive, we retain all rights to all control, income and profits of the trust property listed on Schedule A of The _____ (your names) Living Trust.

1. So long as _____ (wife's name) is alive, she shall retain all rights to all income, profits, and control of her separate property listed on Schedule B of The _____ Living Trust.

2. So long as _____ (husband's name) is alive, he shall retain all rights to all income, profits, and control of his separate property listed on Schedule C of The _____ (your names) Living Trust.

SAMPLE AB DISCLAIMER LIVING TRUST

C. Additional or Property Acquired After Establishment of the Trust

Property may be added to the trust at any time by either grantor, or both.

D. Character of Property Placed in Trust

Property transferred to this trust shall keep its original character while both of us are alive. If revocation of the trust is invoked, the trustee shall distribute the trust property to us based on the same ownership rights we had before the property was transferred to the trust. Specifically:

1. Shared Property

All trust property listed on Schedule A was shared property. Note: Identify character of Schedule A listed property in spaces below.

_____

_____

_____

2. Separate Property

The trust property listed on Schedule B shall retain its character as the separate property of _____ (wife's name). The trust property listed on Schedule C shall retain its character as the separate property of _____ _____ (husband's name).

E. Revocation

For as long as both of us live, either one of us may revoke The _____ Living Trust at any time by writing given to the other grantor, except as provided otherwise in this document. No beneficiary need be given any notice of revocation.

SAMPLE AB DISCLAIMER LIVING TRUST

F. Amendment

Except as provided otherwise in this document, The _____ Living Trust may be altered, amended, or modified only by a writing signed by both of us, as grantors. After the death of a spouse, the surviving spouse can amend his or her revocable living trust, except as provided otherwise in this document.

G. Residence Rights

As grantors, we retain the right to possess and occupy our principal residence for life, rent-free and without charge with the exception of insurance, maintenance, taxes and related costs and expenses.

Article III. Trustees

A. Original Trustees

The trustees of The _____ Living Trust and any AB trust or other trust, including any child's trust created under this Declaration of Trust shall be _____ (your names). Either trustee may act for, and represent, the trust, in any transaction.

B. Trustee on Death or Incapacity of Original Trustee

Upon the death or incapacity of _____ (wife's name) or _____ (husband's name), the other spouse shall serve as sole trustee of this trust and all trusts and any child's trust created under this Declaration of Trust.

C. Trustee's Responsibility

The trustee in office shall serve as trustee of this trust and all trusts and any child's trust created under this Declaration of Trust.

SAMPLE AB DISCLAIMER LIVING TRUST

D. Terminology

In this Declaration of Trust, the term "trustee" includes any successor trustee or trustees.

E. Successor Trustee

Upon the death or incapacity of the surviving spouse, or the incapacity of both spouses, the successor trustee shall be ___

_____ _____

_____ (name or names). If they are unable to serve or to continue serving as successor trustee, the next successor trustee(s) shall be

_____ (name).

_____ (name).

_____ (name).

Any of the successor trustees has full and independent authority to act for and represent the trust. They must all consent in writing to any transaction involving the trust or trust property,

F. Trustee Resignation

At any time, any trustee in office may resign by signing and submitting a notice of resignation. The resignation must be delivered to the person or institution that is either named in this Declaration of Trust or appointed by the trustee.

G. Power to Appoint Successor Trustee

If all the successor trustees cease to, or are unable to, serve as trustee, the last acting trustee may appoint an additional successor trustee or trustees to serve in the order nominated. The appointment must be made in writing, signed by the trustee, and notarized.

H. Waiver of Bond

SAMPLE AB DISCLAIMER LIVING TRUST

No bond shall be required of any trustee.

I. Compensation

No trustee shall receive any compensation for serving as trustee. Exceptions: A trustee shall be entitled to reasonable compensation, as determined by the trustee, for serving as a trustee of Trust A, or a child's trust created by this Declaration of Trust, or for serving as trustee because one or both of us have become incapacitated.

J. Trustee Liability

In the exercise or non-exercise of discretionary powers granted by this Declaration of Trust, the trustee shall not be liable for actions taken in good faith.

Article IV. Specific Beneficiaries

A. Wife's Specific and Alternate Beneficiaries

Upon the death of _____ (wife's name), the following gifts shall be made from trust property owned by _____ (wife's name).

1. _____ (beneficiary's name/ names) shall be given _____ (identify property). In the event, _____ (beneficiary) does not survive _____ (wife's name), that property shall be given to _____ (alternate beneficiary).

2. _____ (beneficiary's name/ names) shall be given _____ (identify property). In the event, _____ (beneficiary) does not survive _____ (wife's name), that property shall be given to _____ (alternate beneficiary).

SAMPLE AB DISCLAIMER LIVING TRUST

3. _____
_____ (beneficiary's name/names) shall be given
_____ (identify property). In the
event, _____ (beneficiary) does not survive
_____ (wife's name), that property
shall be given to _____
(alternate beneficiary).

B. Husband's Specific and Alternate Beneficiaries

Upon the death of _____
(husband's name), the following gifts shall be made from trust
property owned by _____
(husband's name).

1. _____
_____ (beneficiary's name/names) shall be given
_____ (identify property). In the
event, _____ (beneficiary) does not survive
_____ (husband's name), that
property shall be given to _____
_____ (alternate beneficiary).

2. _____
_____ (beneficiary's name/names) shall be given
_____ (identify property). In the
event, _____ (beneficiary) does not survive
_____ (husband's name), that
property shall be given to _____
_____ (alternate beneficiary).

3. _____
_____ (beneficiary's name/names) shall be given
_____ (identify property). In the
event, _____ (beneficiary) does not survive
_____ (husband's name), that
property shall be given to _____
_____ (alternate beneficiary).

SAMPLE AB DISCLAIMER LIVING TRUST

C. Remaining Trust Property

All other trust property of the deceased spouse shall be transferred and administered, as provided for in this document.

Article V. Division of Trust Property Upon First Death

A. Terminology

1. The first grantor to die shall be called the "deceased spouse." The living grantor shall then be called the "surviving spouse."

2. The "trust property of the deceased spouse" shall consist of all property of The _____ Living Trust individually owned by the deceased spouse at the time it was transferred to the trustee. In addition, this includes shared ownership property with a total value equal to _____ of the total value (at the time of the deceased spouse's death) of the shared ownership trust property. This includes:

   _____

   _____

   _____

   _____

   (E.g., accumulated income, appreciation in value, and the like, attributable to the ownership interest of the deceased spouse, etc.)

3. The "trust property of the surviving spouse" shall consist of all property of The _____ Living Trust individually owned by the surviving spouse at the time it was transferred to the trustee, plus shared ownership property with a total value equal to _____ of the total value at the time of the deceased spouse's death of the shared ownership trust property. This includes:

SAMPLE AB DISCLAIMER LIVING TRUST

_____

_____

_____

(E.g., accumulated income, appreciation in value, and the like, attributable to the ownership interest of the surviving spouse, etc.)

B. Division of Trust Assets

After the death of the deceased spouse, the trustee shall divide the trust assets into three shares, called the Survivor's Share, the Marital Deduction Share, and the Bypass Trust Share.

1. Survivor's Share. This share consists of the trust assets of the surviving spouse, as defined in Section A. These assets shall be held in and administered as part of Trust B, the Surviving Spouse's Trust.

2. Marital Deduction Share. This share consists of the assets that pass to the surviving spouse under this declaration of trust that are not disclaimed by the surviving spouse within ___ months of the deceased spouse's death. These assets shall be held in and administered as part of Trust B.

3. The Bypass Trust Share. This share consists of assets that pass to the surviving spouse under this Declaration of Trust that are disclaimed by the surviving spouse. The assets shall be held and administered in Trust A, the Deceased Spouse's Trust.

C. Disclaimer of Trust Assets

The surviving spouse has the authority to disclaim any trust assets left to him or her by the deceased spouse. The surviving spouse is not required to disclaim any of these trust assets. If the surviving spouse chooses to disclaim property, he or she shall do so within _____ months after the deceased spouse's

SAMPLE AB DISCLAIMER LIVING TRUST

death. Any disclaimed property shall be called the "Bypass Trust Share," and shall be held and administered in Trust A. If the surviving spouse does not disclaim any assets left to him or her by the deceased spouse's trust, the trustee shall not establish Trust A.

D. Property of Trust A

1. If the trustee does establish Trust A, that trust shall contain all assets disclaimed by the surviving spouse.

2. The deceased spouse's trust property placed in Trust A shall exclude any specific gifts as provided for in this document.

3. The trustee shall exclusively determine what records, documents, and actions are required to establish and maintain Trust A and Trust B.

E. Administration of Trust A

All property held in Trust A shall be administered as follows:

1. Upon the establishment of Trust A, that trust shall be irrevocable.

2. The life beneficiary of Trust A shall be the surviving spouse.

3. If _____ (wife's name) is the deceased spouse, the final beneficiaries of Trust A shall be: _____. If _____ _____ (wife's name) is the deceased spouse, the alternate final beneficiaries of Trust A shall be: _ _____.

4. If _____ (husband's name) is the deceased spouse, the final beneficiaries of Trust A shall be: _____. If _____ _____ (husband's name) is the deceased spouse, the alternate final beneficiaries of Trust A shall be: _____.

SAMPLE AB DISCLAIMER LIVING TRUST

5. The trustee shall pay to or spend for the benefit of the surviving spouse the net income of Trust A at least _____ (monthly, quarterly, etc.). The trustee shall also pay to or spend for the surviving spouse's benefit any sums from the principal of Trust A necessary for the surviving spouse's education, health, maintenance and support in accordance with his or her accustomed manner of living.

6. No accounting of Trust A shall be required of the trustee, except that the final beneficiaries shall be provided with copies of the annual federal income tax return.

7. The trustee shall be entitled to reasonable compensation from assets of Trust A for services rendered for management of Trust A without court approval.

8. Upon the death of the life beneficiary, the trustee shall distribute the property of Trust A to the final or alternate final beneficiary or beneficiaries, as specified in this document.

Article VI. Trust B, The Surviving Spouse's Trust

A. Creation of Trust B

Upon the death of the deceased spouse, all trust property owned by the surviving spouse, as defined in this document, shall be held in Trust B. Trust B shall include any trust property of the deceased spouse left to the surviving spouse and not disclaimed by her or him.

B. Administration of Trust B

Until the death of the surviving spouse, the surviving spouse retains all rights to all control, income, and profits of the property in Trust B. At any time, the surviving spouse may amend or revoke Trust B during his or her lifetime, without notifying any beneficiary.

C. Distribution of Property in Trust B

SAMPLE AB DISCLAIMER LIVING TRUST

1. Upon the death of the surviving spouse, Trust B becomes irrevocable.

2. The trustee shall first distribute any specific gifts of the surviving spouse to the beneficiaries as named in this document. The trustee shall then distribute all remaining property of Trust B to the final, or alternate final, beneficiary or beneficiaries, as named in this document.

3. All distributions are subject to any provision in this Declaration of Trust that creates child's trusts or creates custodianships under the Uniform Transfers to Minors Act.

Article VII. Incapacity

A. Incapacity of Grantors

If both of us, as grantors, become physically or mentally incapacitated and are no longer able to manage this trust, the successor trustee(s) shall serve as trustee. The determination of the grantors' capacity to manage this trust shall be made by those of the persons listed below who are reasonably available when the successor trustee(s) requests their opinion. If a majority of these persons state in writing that in their opinion the grantors are no longer reasonably capable of serving as trustee, the successor trustee shall serve as trustee.

_____

_____

_____

The successor trustee shall pay trust income at least _____ (monthly, quarterly, annually, etc.) to, or for the benefit of, the grantors and may also spend any amount of trust principal necessary, in the successor trustee's discretion, for the needs of the grantors, until the grantors or either of them are no longer incapacitated or until their deaths.

SAMPLE AB DISCLAIMER LIVING TRUST

B. If Estate Tax Law changes, Amendment of AB Trust

Not withstanding any other provision of this trust, if Congress changes the estate tax law, this trust may be amended as follows:

1. If both grantors are alive but one is incapacitated, the competent spouse may amend this AB trust in order to take best advantage of the new tax law.

2. If both grantors are alive but incapacitated, the successor trustee may amend this AB trust in order to take best advantage of the new tax law.

C. Incapacity of Surviving Spouse

If, after the death of the deceased spouse, the surviving spouse becomes physically or mentally incapacitated and is no longer able to manage Trust B, the person or persons named as successor trustee shall serve as trustee.

1. The determination of the grantor's capacity to manage the trust shall be made by those of the persons listed below who are reasonably available when the successor trustee(s) requests their opinion. If a majority of these persons state in writing that, in their opinion, the grantor is no longer reasonably capable of serving as trustee, the successor trustee shall serve as trustee.

_____

_____

_____

2. The successor trustee shall pay trust income at least _____ (monthly, quarterly, annually, etc) to, or for the benefit of, the surviving spouse. He or she may spend any amount of that trust's principal necessary in the successor trustee's discretion, for the needs of the surviving spouse, until the surviving spouse is no longer incapacitated, or until

SAMPLE AB DISCLAIMER LIVING TRUST

his or her death. Any income not spent for the benefit of the surviving spouse shall be accumulated and added to the property of Trust B.

3. The successor trustee shall manage Trust A, until the surviving spouse is again able to manage his or her own affairs and is able to serve as trustee of that trust, or until the death of the surviving spouse.

4. The successor trustee shall manage any operational child's trust created by their Declaration of Trust.

Article VIII. Simultaneous Death

If both of us, as grantors, should die simultaneously, or under such circumstances as to render it difficult or impossible to determine who predeceased the other, for the purposes of this living trust, it shall be conclusively presumed that both of us died at the same moment. Neither shall be presumed to have survived the other. Upon that event, the trustee shall make any specific gifts left by either spouse, and then distribute all remaining property to each spouse's final beneficiaries.

Article IX. Trustee's Powers and Duties

A. Powers Under State Law

To carry out the provisions of this Declaration of Trust and to manage the trust property of The _____ (your names) Living Trust, Trust A, and Trust B, and any child's trust created under this Declaration of Trust, the trustee shall have all authority and power allowed or conferred under _____ (state name) law, subject to the rights retained by each grantor in this document and to the trustee's fiduciary duty to the grantors and the beneficiaries.

B. Specified Powers

The trustee's powers include, but are not limited to:

SAMPLE AB DISCLAIMER LIVING TRUST

1. The power to sell trust and manage property, and to borrow money and to encumber property, specifically including:

_____

_____

_____

(E.g., the power to lease, grant options to lease the property, to make repairs or alterations, to insure against loss, etc.)

3. The power to sell or grant options for the sale or exchange of any trust property, including:

_____

_____

_____

(E.g., bonds, debentures, stocks, and any other form of security or security account)

4. The power to invest and diversify trust property in property of any kind, including:

_____

_____

_____

(E.g., bonds, debentures, mortgages, notes, stocks, stock options, stock futures, buying on margin, etc.)

5. The power to receive additional property from any source and add to any trust created by this Declaration of Trust.

6. The power to employ and pay reasonable fees to accountants, investment experts, or lawyers, for information or advice relating to the trust.

7. The power to continue any business of either grantor.

8. The power to institute or defend legal actions involving the trust or the grantors' affairs.

SAMPLE AB DISCLAIMER LIVING TRUST

9. The power to execute any documents necessary to administer any trust created in this Declaration of Trust.

C. Payment by the Trustee of the Grantors' Debts and Taxes

1. Wife's Debts and Taxes _____ __
___ _____ (wife's name) debts and death taxes shall be paid by the trustee. The trustee shall pay these from the following trust property:

_____

_____

_____

2. Husband's Debts and Taxes _____
_____'s (husband's name) debts and death taxes shall be paid by the trustee. The trustee shall pay these from the following trust property:

_____

_____

_____

3. If Specified Property Insufficient. If the property described above is insufficient to pay all of our debts and death taxes, the trustee shall determine how such debts and death taxes shall be paid from that grantor's trust property, except as limited by any law or IRS regulation controlling the property in Trust A.

Article X. General Administrative Provisions

A. Controlling Law

The validity of The _____ Living Trust and construction of its provisions shall be governed by the laws of _____ (state name).

B. Severability

SAMPLE AB DISCLAIMER LIVING TRUST

If any provision of this Declaration of Trust is ruled unenforceable, the remaining provisions shall nevertheless remain in effect.

C. Amendments

The term "Declaration of Trust" includes any provisions added by valid amendment.

Article XI. Child's Trusts

All trust property left to any of the minor or young adult beneficiaries listed below shall be retained in trust for each such beneficiary in a separate trust of this _____ Living Trust. Each trust may be identified and referred to by adding the name of that trust's beneficiary to the name of this trust. The following terms apply to each child's trust:

A. Trust Beneficiaries and Age Limits

A child's trust shall end when the beneficiary of that trust, listed below, becomes _____ (age), except as otherwise specified in this section.

Name(s) of Beneficiary   Age

_____

_____

_____

B. Powers and Duties of Child's Trust Trustee

1. Until a child's trust ends, the trustee may distribute to or use for the benefit of the beneficiary as much of the net income or principal of the child's trust as the trustee deems necessary for the beneficiary's education, health, maintenance, and support. Education includes, but is not limited to:

_____

_____

_____

SAMPLE AB DISCLAIMER LIVING TRUST

(E.g. college, graduate, postgraduate, and vocational studies, and education-related living expenses.)

2. In deciding whether or not to make a distribution to the beneficiary, the trustee may take into account the beneficiary's other income, resources, and sources of support.

3. Any child's trust income not distributed to a beneficiary by the trustee shall be accumulated and added to the principal of the trust for that beneficiary.

4. The trustee of a child's trust is not required to make any accounting or report to the trust beneficiary.

C. Prohibition of Assignment of Interest of Beneficiary

The interests of a child's trust beneficiary shall not be transferable by voluntary or involuntary assignment or by operation of law before actual receipt by the beneficiary. These interests shall be free from the claims of creditors and from attachments, bankruptcy, execution, or any other legal process to the fullest extent permitted by law.

D. Trustee Compensation

Any trustee of a child's trust created shall be entitled to reasonable compensation without court approval out of the trust assets for ordinary and extraordinary services. This includes compensation for all services performed in connection with the termination of any trust.

E. Termination of Child's Trusts

A child's trust shall end when any of the following events occurs:

1. The beneficiary reaches the specified age. If the trust ends for this reason, all remaining principal and accumulated income of the trust shall be given outright to the beneficiary.

SAMPLE AB DISCLAIMER LIVING TRUST

   2. The beneficiary dies. If the trust ends for this reason, the trust property shall pass to the beneficiary's heirs.

   3. Under the provisions of this Declaration of Trust, the trustee distributes all trust property.

Article XII. Custodianships Under the Uniform Transfers to Minors Act

A. All property _____ (beneficiary) becomes entitled to under this trust document shall be given to _____ (custodian's name) as custodian for _____ (beneficiary) under the _____ (name of state) Uniform Transfers to Minors Act, until _____ (beneficiary) reaches age _____ .

B. All property _____ (beneficiary) becomes entitled to under this trust document shall be given to _____ (custodian's name) as custodian for _____ (beneficiary) under the _____ (name of state) Uniform Transfers to Minors Act, until _____ (beneficiary) reaches age _____ .

C. All property _____ (beneficiary) becomes entitled to under this trust document shall be given to _____ (custodian's name) as custodian for _____ (beneficiary) under the _____ (name of state) Uniform Transfers to Minors Act, until _____ (beneficiary) reaches age _____ .

D. All property _____ (beneficiary) becomes entitled to under this trust document shall be given to _____ (custodian's name) as

SAMPLE AB DISCLAIMER LIVING TRUST

custodian for _____ (beneficiary) under the _____ (name of state) Uniform Transfers to Minors Act, until _____ (beneficiary) reaches age _____.

Grantors Certification

We certify that we have read this Declaration of Trust. We certify that it correctly states the terms and conditions under which the trust property is to be held, managed and disposed of by the trustees, and we approve the Declaration of Trust.

Dated: _____

_____

Grantor and Trustee

Dated: _____

Notary's Acknowledgment and Declaration

State of _____

County of _____

On _____, 20_____, before me, _____, a notary public in and for said state, personally appeared _____ _____, personally known to me (or proved to me on the basis of satisfactory evidence) to be the persons whose names are subscribed to the within this Declaration of Trust, and acknowledged to me that they executed the same in their authorized capacities and that by their signatures on the instrument they executed the Declaration of Trust.

_____

Signature of Notary   Public

SAMPLE AB DISCLAIMER LIVING TRUST

Schedule A--Shared Property Placed In Trust

_____

_____

_____

_____

_____

_____

Schedule B--Wife's Separate Property Placed In Trust

_____

_____

_____

_____

_____

Schedule C--Husband's Separate Property Placed In Trust

_____

_____

_____

_____

_____

DURABLE HEALTH CARE POWER OF ATTORNEY & ADVANCED HEALTH CARE DIRECTIVE INSTRUCTIONS/LIVING WILL

PART I

Durable Health Care Power of Attorney

I,_____, of_____
_____ (name of county and state) appoint the following person to be my health care agent to make health and personal care decisions for me:

Health Care Agent_____

(Name and relationship)

Address:_____

Telephone Number:

Home_____

Work_____

Email:_____

This document is effective immediately and continuously until my death or until it is revoked in writing signed by me or someone authorized to make health care treatment decisions for me.

I authorize all health care providers or other specified individuals or entities to disclose to my health care agent, upon his or her request, any and all written or oral information in regard to my physical or mental health.

This includes, but is not limited to:

_____

_____

_____

_____

(E.g., medical and hospital records, privileged or personal information, etc.)

DURABLE HEALTH CARE POWER OF ATTORNEY & ADVANCED HEALTH CARE DIRECTIVE INSTRUCTIONS/LIVING WILL

The remainder of this document will take effect when and only when I lack the ability to understand, make, or communicate a choice regarding a health or personal care decision as verified by my attending physician. My health care agent may not delegate the authority to make decisions. My health care agent has all of the following powers subject to the health care treatment instructions that follow in Part II.

PART II

Health Care Treatment Instructions

(Note: Cross out any powers below that you do not want to give your health care agent.)

1. To authorize, withhold, or withdraw:

_____

_____

_____

_____

(E.g. Medical care and surgical procedures; withholding or withdrawal of nutrition (food) or hydration (water) medically supplied by tube through my nose, stomach, intestines, arteries, or veins.

- · To authorize my admission to/discharge from a medical, nursing, residential or similar facility.

- · To make agreements for my care and health insurance for my care, including hospice and/or palliative care.

- · To hire and discharge fire medical, social service and other support personnel responsible for my care.

- · To take any legal action necessary to do what I have directed.

- · To request that a physician responsible for my care issue a do-not-resuscitate (DNR) order to and sign any required documents and consent forms.

DURABLE HEALTH CARE POWER OF ATTORNEY & ADVANCED HEALTH CARE DIRECTIVE INSTRUCTIONS/LIVING WILL

Appointment of Alternate Health Care Agent(s)

If my health care agent is not readily available or if my health care agent is my spouse and an action for divorce is filed by either of us after the date of this document, I appoint the person or persons named below in the order named.

First Alternative Health Care Agent:_____

(Name and relationship)

Address: _____

Telephone Number:

Home_____

Work_____

Email: _____

Second Alternative Health Care Agent: _____

(Name and relationship)

Address: _____

Telephone Number:

Home_____

Work_____

Email: _____

Second Alternative Health Care Agent: _____

Guidance for Health Care Agent(s)

If I have an end-stage medical condition or other irreversible medical condition, my goals in making medical decisions are as follows:

_____

_____

_____

DURABLE HEALTH CARE POWER OF ATTORNEY & ADVANCED HEALTH CARE DIRECTIVE INSTRUCTIONS/LIVING WILL

(E.g., brain disease, severe brain damage, etc. In this section, you can specify what care you want to avoid in the event of such disease or damage; for example, aggressive medical care that might prolong your life, but might also extend your suffering.)

PART III

Living Will

I wish to make my own health care decisions. Therefore, the following instructions are intended to provide clear and convincing evidence of my wishes to be followed when I lack the capacity to understand, make, or communicate my treatment decisions:

If I have an end-stage medical condition (which will result in my death, despite the introduction or continuation of medical treatment) or I am permanently unconscious such as in an irreversible coma or irreversible vegetative state and there is no realistic hope of significant recovery, all of the following apply (cross out any treatment instructions with which you do not agree):

1. I direct that I be given health care treatment to relieve pain or provide comfort even if such treatment might shorten my life, suppress my appetite or my breathing, or be habit forming.

2. I direct that all life prolonging procedures be withheld or withdrawn.

3. I specifically do not want any of the following used as life prolonging procedures:

__ Heart-lung resuscitation (CPR) _____

__ Mechanical ventilator (breathing machine) _____

__ Dialysis (kidney machine) _____

__ Surgery _____

__ Chemotherapy radiation treatment _____

__ Antibiotics _____

DURABLE HEALTH CARE POWER OF ATTORNEY & ADVANCED HEALTH CARE DIRECTIVE INSTRUCTIONS/LIVING WILL

Please indicate whether you want nutrition (food) or hydration (water) medically supplied by a tube into your nose, stomach, intestine, arteries, or veins in the event you have an end-stage medical condition or are permanently unconscious and there is no realistic hope of significant recovery.

Tube Feedings

_____ Yes, I want tube feedings to be given.

_____ No, I do not want tube feedings to be given.

Health Care Agent's Use of Instructions

(Initial one option only)

_____ My health care agent must follow these instructions.

_____ These instructions are only guidance.

I direct that my health care agent shall have final say and may override any of my instructions with the exception of:

_____

_____

_____

Legal Protection for Health Care Agent and Health Care Providers

_____ (name of state) law protects my health care agent and health care providers from any legal liability for their good faith actions in following my wishes as expressed in this document. On behalf of myself, my executors and heirs, I also hold my health care agent and my health care providers harmless and indemnify them against any claim for their good faith actions.

Organ Donation

(Initial One Option Only)

_____ I consent to donate my organs and tissues at the time of my death for the purpose of transplant, medical study, or education.

DURABLE HEALTH CARE POWER OF ATTORNEY & ADVANCED HEALTH CARE DIRECTIVE INSTRUCTIONS/LIVING WILL

_____ I do not consent to donate my organs or tissues at the time of my death.

Having carefully read this document, I have signed it this _____ day of_____, 20__, revoking all previous health care powers of attorney and health care treatment instructions.

Signed: _____

WITNESS: _____

WITNESS: _____

Notarization

On this _____ day of _____, 20____, before me personally appeared the aforesaid declarant, known to me to be the person who executed the foregoing instrument and who acknowledged that he/she executed the same as his/her free act and deed.

IN WITNESS WHEREOF, I have hereunto set my hand and affixed my official seal in the County of_____, State of_____ the day and year first above written.

_____

Notary Public

My commission expires _____

ASSIGNMENT OF BUSINESS INTEREST

I, the undersigned _____ (name of Assignor) hereby assign and transfer to the _____ (name of Assignor's trust) on _____(day, month, year) the following:

All of my interest, right and title as well as all money, funds or profits due, or to become due, to Assignor, derived from the business known as _____(name of business) which is located at _____ (address of business).

I further agree to the following:

1. I have the full legal right and authority to execute and carry out the terms of this Assignment. I certify that, as of the date of the execution of this Assignment, I am not in default in the performance of any obligations existing in regard to _____ (name of business).

2. _____ (name of trust) shall not be liable to any person(s) for damages incurred in connection with _____ (name of business) or any other such contract into which I may have entered into connection thereof.

3. I shall execute and deliver any other instruments which the _____(name of trust) specifies as necessary to carry out the purpose and spirit of this Assignment and to better secure the payment of the liabilities.

4. This Assignment of Business Interest shall be governed by and interpreted in accordance with the laws of _____ (name of state).

This Assignment of Business Interest is binding upon and inures to the _____ (name of trust) and to any holder of the liabilities and is binding upon me.

ASSIGNMENT OF BUSINESS INTEREST

IN WITNESS THEREOF, _____ (name) has executed this Assignment of Business Interest in _____ (name of city), _____ (name of state) on _____ (date, day), 20__.

_____

(Signature of Assignor)

State of _____ (name of state)

County of _____ (name of county)

Notarization

Before me personally appeared the aforesaid Assignor, to me known to be the person described in and who executed the foregoing Assignment and acknowledged that he/she executed the same as his/her free act and deed.

IN WITNESS WHEREOF, I have hereunto set my hand and affixed my official seal in the County of_____, State of_____ the day and year first above written.

_____

Notary Public

My commission expires _____ (date)

Glossary

AB Trust: A trust is one that establishes two trusts, one for each spouse. The surviving spouse can then use the property in the other's trust, but avoids double taxation on the property from when one spouse dies to when the second spouse dies.

Acceleration: The passing of property to a remainderman due to failure by death, remarriage or other means of the preceding beneficiary.

Accumulated Income: A portion of the income in a trust that is retained for future payments to beneficiaries or future use.

Active Trust: A trust that requires activity by the trustee, such as managing investments.

Adjudication: Approval by a court for an accounting or a requested distribution by a trust or an estate.

Administrator: Also called the personal representative. The person or entity responsible for keeping accurate accounting records of trust income, expenses and assets, process distributions, and assisting the trustee and complying with state and federal tax laws.

Advancement: A gift to children or heirs which is made in expectation of a gift to come from the still-living parent's potential estate. Gift is made as an advance on the child or heir's inheritance.

Aliquot: an explicit partial share which is generally applied when dividing and distributing an estate or trust assets.

Amendment: A formally executed document that amends the terms of a trust from the previously executed trust instrument.

Annual Valuation Date: The date each year that the trustee must value the trust assets for purposes of determining the annual unitrust amount.

Annuity: A series of payments at regular intervals for a number of years or over a person's lifetime.

Appraisal: The valuation of a property.

Beach Bum Trust Provision: This is a condition of a trust that an heir or beneficiary may only receive the money from the trust equal to the amount earned by the beneficiary. This encourages the beneficiary to work and not live on just the trust profits alone.

Beneficiary: An individual who is to benefit from an established trust or will. Either a present beneficiary or a future beneficiary, called a remainderman.

Bond: Insurance that pledges funds to replace trust assets misappropriated by a trustee.

Breach of Trust: This is an act that violates the duties of the trustee or the trust's terms. This breach does not necessarily need to be on purpose or out of spite; negligence is considered a breach of trust.

Burial Trust: Provides the funds necessary to cover the cost of your burial (or cremation) arrangements; this can be a revocable trust, but after your death it becomes irrevocable and the trust cannot be used for anything else.

Bypass Trust: A trust set up to bypass the surviving spouse's estate, thereby allowing full use of the applicable exclusion amount for both spouses.

Charitable Lead Trust: A gift agreement providing income to a charity for a term of certain years and the remaining principal either returns to the donor or a designee of the donor.

Charitable Remainder Trust: The general term used to describe a separate trust arrangement between the donor and the trustee. Income is paid to an individual over time, usually the lifetime of the beneficiary, with the remainder paid to a charitable organization.

Charitable Trust: An irrevocable trust where the current or future beneficiary is a charitable organization. These trusts can offer significant income tax, estate tax, and capital gains tax benefits.

Child's Trust: A trust that is created solely for the use of one child who is a minor.

Community Property: Ownership between a husband and wife, available in certain states. Laws vary by state, but the basic rule is that all property earned or acquired by either spouse during marriage (except for gifts or inheritances received by either spouse) is treated as owned one-half by each spouse.

Constructive Trust: This trust occurs when a person has a title to or takes possession of a property under the circumstances that they are only holding it for another person. There is no formal trust document or agreement for this.

Corpus: Principal or capital of an estate or trust.

Co-trustee: When there is more than one trustee of a trust serving at the same time, they are co-trustees. Co-trustees will have the same powers and obligations. A co-trustee may be only temporary while the original trustee is unavailable due to sickness or other serious matter.

Credit Shelter Trust: A trust funded with the Unified Credit Exemption Equivalent amount. It avoids taxation of the amount and any appreciation upon the death of the surviving spouse. See Bypass Trust.

Crummey Trust: A complicated trust set up in conjunction with an irrevocable life insurance trust to make the payments for a life insurance policy; this is the kind of trust that requires an estate-planning attorney.

Decedent: A deceased person.

Declaration of Trust: This is the document which a trustor signs to create the trust in which the person's assets will be placed.

Deed of Trust: For the states: Alaska, Arizona, California, Colorado, Georgia, Idaho, Illinois, Mississippi, Missouri, Montana, North Carolina, Texas, Virginia and West Virginia. This is a document used in place of a mortgage which guarantees real property to secure a loan.

Descendant: An individual who is descended in direct line from another.

Deferred Charitable Gift Annuity: A charitable gift annuity contract where the income is deferred until a specified time by the contract.

Designated Beneficiary Plan: This is also known as Pay on Death Account, Transfer on Death Account, or Totten Trust. It allows a person to choose beneficiaries and specify what percentage of account assets will be left to each one. The assets are excluded from the probate process.

Discretionary Trust: A trust with provisions to give the trustee the authority to pay income or principal to or for the benefit of the beneficiaries at the trustee's discretion.

Domicile: A person's permanent home or residence, though not necessarily where the person lives.

Donee: A person or entity that receives a gift.

Donor: A person who makes a charitable contribution outright to charity or to a trust for the benefit of charity.

Dynasty Trust: Also known as a wealth trust, can last for several generations or be set up to never end. This kind of trust helps people with a vast amount of wealth control the distribution of that money and property over many years.

Educational Trust: This is a kind of protective trust that sets aside money specifically for education-related expenses — tuition or training fees, books, supplies; these trusts usually include provisions to stop payments if the student drops out of school or fails a lot of classes.

Estate: Everything a person owns of value, such as life insurance, investments, cars, jewelry, and collectibles less any debts owed on that property.

Estate Tax: Tax on the value of the estate an individual leaves upon death. It is often called an inheritance tax or death tax.

Exemption Equivalent: The amount whose gift or estate tax is equal to the Unified Credit and can be given away during the lifetime or at death without transfer tax.

Exemption Amount: The equivalent amount of assets that can be transferred free of tax, either during life or at death, by using the Applicable Credit Amount when calculating estate and gift taxes.

Family Trust: A legal arrangement that involves the transfer of property from the original owner to a family member for the purpose of holding and maintaining the property until the beneficiary takes ownership.

Fiduciary: A person or legal entity acting on behalf of a trustee, personal representative, guardian, conservator, or agent under a power of attorney.

Funding a Trust: The placement of property in a trust; that same property will be called "trust principal" when it is under the auspices of the trust agreement.

Generation Skipping Tax Transfer (GSTT): This is a federal tax levied on property transferred to a person one or more generations removed from the donor.

Generation Skipping Transfer Trust: A tax-saving trust that is designed to benefit multiple generations after you're gone.

Gift Tax: A tax imposed on transfers of property by gifts during the donor's lifetime.

Grantor: Also known as the trustor. This is the person who creates the trust and decides what property to include in the trust and who the beneficiaries will be. This person may make changes to the trust as long as they are alive; after that time it becomes an irrevocable trust and cannot be changed.

Grantor-Retained Trusts: These are irrevocable, non-charitable trusts. This means they are set up in a way similar to a charitable trust but the beneficiary is not a charity. There are three common types.

Grantor-Retained Annuity Trust (GRAT): Gives a fixed amount of money at predetermined times, usually at regularly scheduled intervals.

Grantor-Retained Incomes Trust (GRIT): Designates specific people to receive certain property — such as stocks or a house — but the income or use of the property stays with you until your death.

Grantor-Retained Unit Trust (GRUT): Pays a specific percentage to the beneficiary.

Income: The return in money or property derived from the use of principal, such as rents, interest, dividends, royalties, and receipts from business operations.

Income Beneficiary: A beneficiary entitled to receive the income from the trust.

Income Recipient: An individual who is entitled to receive unitrust amount payments from a CRT. A charity can be an income recipient but only if there is at least one other non-charitable income recipient named.

Independent Special Trustee: A special trustee who is chosen to act independently of the trustee. Independent special trustees are often required for a CRT when the primary trustee will be the trustmaker or a party who is related or subordinate to the trustmaker.

Inheritance Tax: A tax levied on the rights of heirs to receive property from a decedent, which is measured by the share passing to each beneficiary.

Intangible Property: Property that does not have physical substance. Examples include certificates of stock or insurance policies.

Inter Vivos: During a person's lifetime, such as an inter vivos trust or living trust.

Irrevocable trust: A trust which the trustor does not have the power to revoke or amend.

Joint Tenancy: When two or more people own property. The other will become the owner of the entire property when one dies.

Legal Title: Legal position that gives the trustee ownership of the property in a trust for the duration of the trustee's responsibility.

Life Insurance Trust: An irrevocable trust established to of exclude life insurance proceeds from the estate of the insured and the spouse of the insured for death tax purposes.

Liquid Assets: Cash or assets that can be converted into cash without any serious loss, such as in bank accounts, life insurance proceeds, or government bonds.

Living Trust: A trust that is created while the grantor is still alive. It can be either revocable and changed during the trustor's lifetime, or irrevocable, which is unchangeable.

Marital Deduction: An estate and gift tax deduction available for property passing to a spouse either during lifetime or at death.

Marital Trust: A separate trust created under a revocable living trust at the grantor's death that qualifies for a marital deduction.

Minor Trust: A way to give gifts to a minor that avoids the gift tax and keeps the property safe until the minor becomes an adult and can take ownership of the trust.

Non-Discretionary Trust: A trust whereby the trustee may only invest in particular securities and is directed to diversify the investments among specific types of securities. The trustee has no power or discretion in the trust.

Passive: This refers to an inactive trustee who has no responsibilities for the trust besides holding the title or waiting for something to happen which would then activate the trust.

Personal Representative: Also called executor. The person appointed in a will or through the court to control and protect an estate's assets.

Power of Attorney: Written document legally authorizing someone to act for another. A durable power of attorney continues to be valid after the person being managed becomes incapacitated.

Principal: The property of an estate or contributed to a trust as distinguished from its income.

Probate: The court proceeding through which a will is verified and executed. If a person dies without a valid will, the probate court will determine the estate's beneficiaries according to state law.

Protective Trusts: Trusts designed with conditions to protect the beneficiary's property.

Qualified Domestic Trust (QDOT): A trust established for a non-U.S. citizen surviving spouse that qualifies for a marital deduction.

Qualified Terminable Interest Property (QTIP) Trust: A trust that qualifies for the marital deduction and allows the deceased spouse to decide on the ultimate disposition of the trust property upon death of the surviving spouse. It avoids any transfer tax upon the death of the first spouse and provides the surviving spouse with income from the property during his or her life.

Real Estate Investment Trust (REIT): A REIT is a company that owns and operates income-producing real estate, including office buildings, hotels, apartments, medical office parks and even, occasionally, a golf course. Other REITs, ones known as mortgage REITS, stick strictly to financing other real estate deals and projects. To qualify as a REIT under the federal guidelines, the company must distribute at least 90 percent of its taxable income to shareholders annually through dividends.

Remainder Interest: The interest that passes to a beneficiary upon the expiration of a period of time in which another beneficiary was entitled to benefits from the property. What remains at the termination of a trust.

Remainderman: The beneficiary entitled to a remainder interest.

Revocable trust: A trust plan that gives the grantor the power to alter the trust terms or revoke the trust.

Schedule: A list of all property included in a trust.

THE COMPLETE GUIDE TO CREATING YOUR OWN LIVING TRUST

Settlor: This is one term for the person who funds a trust. This person is also called a grantor.

Separate Property: Everything that a husband and wife own separately of one another.

Share: Generally an equal fraction of a benefit from a trust with others. (For example, "to my four sons, in equal shares").

Share and Share Alike: Refers to the act of dividing a gift equally among beneficiaries

Simple Trust: This type of trust requires that all income be distributed each year and it may not be accrued.

Special Needs Trust: A support trust for a disabled person.

Spendthrift Trust: A trust that is set up for someone who will not be able to handle his own affairs — someone who is mentally incompetent or someone who might have financial problems and needs protection from creditors. The beneficiary does not own the property in the trust, just the payments that are made from the trust.

Split-Interest Trust: More than one individual benefits from the trust: one person or charity would have an interest in the trust for a specific period of time, and then another person or charity receives the property that remains.

Statutory Share: Refers to the amount of a deceased spouse's estate that the surviving spouse is entitled to. This amount is typically one-third or one-half of the estate, but can vary among states.

Successor Trustee: A person who follows and assumes the responsibilities of a prior trustee as provided for in the trust instrument.

Supplemental Needs Trust: A support trust for a handicapped, elderly, or disabled person in need of support is assisted by this trust in such a way that it doesn't reduce or jeopardize the eligibility of that person to receive public or private benefits. This trust is designed to protect your property from seizure by the government or a creditor seeking reimbursement.

Support Trust: Requires a trustee to pay only the income and property necessary to cover the cost of education or assistance (such as health care or nursing home fees) of the beneficiaries.

Tangible Property: Property that can be touched. Jewelry, furniture, automobiles are examples of tangible property.

Taxable Estate: The adjusted gross income minus the marital deduction or charitable deduction.

Tenancy-in-Common: Joint ownership by two or more persons who own interest in the same property. At the death of one person, ownership transfers to that person's designated beneficiaries or heirs, not to the other joint owner or owners.

Testamentary Trust: A provision under a will that establishes a trust. The trust does not take effect until the death of the person who created the will.

Totten Trust: A bank account that upon your death immediately passes to the named beneficiary.

Trust: A legal arrangement where the creator transfers legal title to property to a trust and names a trustee to manage the property for the benefit of a person or beneficiaries.

Trust Agreement: A written document outlining the terms of a trust arrangement. Also called a trust document or trust instrument.

Trustee: A person, bank or trust company with the title to trust property and charged with managing the property in accordance with the terms of the trust document for the benefit of beneficiaries named to the trust.

Trustor: The person who creates the trust and owns property that will be put in the trust. Also called grantor, settlor, or creator.

Trust Principal: The name given to property that is placed into a trust and is managed by a trust agreement.

Trust Term: The time during which the trustee holds the trust property for the benefit of the beneficiaries and the charitable remainderman.

Unified Tax Credit: Describes the combined estate and gift tax credit that permits the transfer of assets free of tax either during lifetime or at death.

Unitrust: A term used to describe a form of charitable remainder trust.

Vested Interest: A fixed interest in real or personal property.

Will: A legal document directing the disposition of property, which is to be operable at the time of death of the person who created the document.

Author Biography

S teven D. Fisher is an independent writer, illustrator, and instructional designer with more than 25 years of experience in business writing and training and development. His specialties include the design and writing of books, certification tests, e-books, manuals, seminars and workshops. In addition to practical "real world" experience, he holds an M.A. in Education of the Hearing Impaired and trained as a print and media Broadcast Specialist in the U.S. Army.

Bibliography

Abts, Henry W. (1999) *How To Settle Your Living Trust: How You Can Settle a Living Trust Swiftly, Easily, and Safely*. New York, New York: McGraw-Hill.

Abts, Henry W. (2002) *The Living Trust: The Failproof Way to Pass Along Your Estate to Your Heirs*, 3rd Edition. New York, New York: McGraw-Hill.

Clifford, Denis. (2005) *Make Your Own Living Trust*, 7th Edition. Berkeley, California: Nolo.

Distenfield, Ira & Distenfield, Linda. (2005) *We The People's Guide to Estate Planning: A Do-It-Yourself Plan for Creating a Will and Living Trust*. Hoboken, New Jersey: John Wiley & Sons, Inc.

Web Resources:

www.fdic.gov
www.kiplinger.com
www.vba.va.gov
www.va.gov
www.irs.gov
www.sec.gov
www.copyright.gov
www.uspto.gov
www.cbsnews.com

Index

THE COMPLETE GUIDE TO LEAVING AN INHERITANCE FOR YOUR CHILDREN AND OTHERS: WHAT YOU NEED TO KNOW EXPLAINED SIMPLY

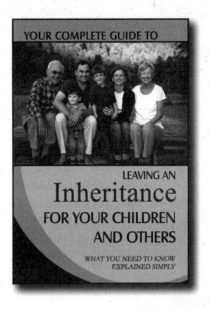

While more than 50 percent of Americans feel it is important to leave an inheritance for their children and other beneficiaries, the majority have not yet made any plans for their estate. This new book will serve as an aid in your planning, providing you with indispensable information and the necessary tools.

In this book, you will learn tips for distributing inheritance among children and what an appropriate inheritance is, as well as about inheritance taxes, exempt beneficiaries, disinheritance, durable power of attorney, and advance health care directives. Additionally, you will learn tips for distributing inheritance among children; what an appropriate inheritance is; how to prevent fights over inherited property; how to deal with adopted children, stepchildren, and children from a second marriage; how to select trustees and guardians; how to protect your money from a financially immature child, a child's spouse, and creditors; how to divide valuables and non-cash assets; and how to deal with the family home.

ISBN-13: 978-1-60138-210-8
288 Pages • $24.95

THE COMPLETE GUIDE TO IRAS & IRA INVESTING: WEALTH BUILDING STRATEGIES REVEALED

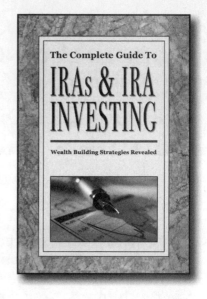

As more and more baby boomers prepare to retire and as people seem to be retiring at an earlier age, the importance of saving for retirement has become increasingly apparent. Many people find themselves worrying that they will not be able to maintain their current life style once they retire. However, the strategies provided in this book will help you turn your IRA into a wealth-building tool.

The Complete Guide to IRAs and IRA Investing will show you how to take control of your investment future and make sure your investments are performing for you. You will learn about Roth IRAs, traditional IRAs, SEP IRAs, SIMPLE IRAs, and self-directed IRAs, and you will learn how to choose the right plan for you. You will learn about the Economic Growth and Tax Relief Reconciliation Act of 2001, rules regarding distribution, rollovers, transfers, conversions between accounts, valid adjustments, adjusted gross income, annual contribution limits, the advantages and disadvantages of the various IRAs, potential penalties, tax deductible contributions, myths and truths about IRA investing, and IRS guidelines.

ISBN-13: 978-1-60138-202-3
288 Pages • $24.95

THE COMPLETE GUIDE TO TRUSTEE ESTATE MANAGEMENT:
WHAT YOU NEED TO KNOW ABOUT BEING AN EXECUTOR EXPLAINED SIMPLY

One of the most critical decisions a person must make when crafting a will is who to name as executor. Being chosen for this important job is an honor, and you must know how to perform the tasks correctly. With the help of this new book, *The Complete Guide to Trustee Estate Management*, you will understand the complex process of carrying out a person's final wishes.

This book will provide insight whether you are a lawyer, accountant, financial consultant, spouse, adult child, relative, or friend; the simple, easy to understand language makes this book accessible to everyone. You will become familiar with many estate management terms, such as beneficiary, probate, remaindermen, trust agreement, trust property, trustor, and trustee.

As executor, you will be responsible for settling the deceased person's estate. Using this book as a guide, you can be assured that you will be prepared to properly perform the necessary duties entrusted to you.

ISBN-13: 978-1-60138-201-6
288 Pages • $24.95

DID YOU BORROW THIS COPY?

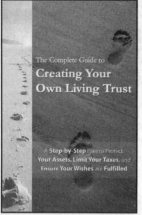